Israel
as a
Religious
Reality

Israel
as a
Religious
Reality

edited by Chaim I. Waxman

The Orthodox Forum Series
A Project of the Rabbi Isaac Elchanan Theological Seminary
An Affiliate of Yeshiva University

JASON ARONSON INC.
Northvale, New Jersey
London

This book was set in 11 pt. Goudy Oldstyle by Alpha Graphics of Pittsfield, New Hampshire, and printed by Haddon Craftsmen, of Scranton, Pennsylvania.

Copyright © 1994 by Rabbi Isaac Elchanan Theological Seminary

10 9 8 7 6 5 4 3 2 1

Library of Congress Cataloging-in-Publication Data

Israel as a religious reality / edited by Chaim I. Waxman.
    p. cm.
    Includes bibliographical references and index.
    ISBN 1-56821-077-9
    1. Palestine in Judaism—Congresses. 2. Orthodox Judaism—United
States—Congresses. 3. Orthodox Judaism—Israel—Congresses.
4. Religious Zionism—Congresses. I. Waxman, Chaim Isaac.
BM729.P3I85   1994
296.3—dc20   93-34029

Manufactured in the United States of America. Jason Aronson Inc. offers books and cassettes. For information and catalog write to Jason Aronson Inc., 230 Livingston Street, Northvale, New Jersey 07647.

THE ORTHODOX FORUM

The Orthodox Forum, convened by Dr. Norman Lamm, President of Yeshiva University, meets each year to consider major issues of concern to the Jewish community. Forum participants from throughout the world, including academicians in both Jewish and secular fields, rabbis, *rashei yeshiva*, Jewish educators, and Jewish communal professionals, gather in conference as a think tank to discuss and critique each other's original papers, examining different aspects of a central theme. The purpose of the Forum is to create and disseminate a new and vibrant Torah literature addressing the critical issues facing Jewry today.

The Orthodox Forum
gratefully acknowledges the support
of the Joseph J. Green Memorial Fund
at the Rabbi Isaac Elchanan Theological Seminary.

THE ORTHODOX FORUM
Third Conference

November 25–26, 1990, 8–9 *Kislev* 5751
Congregation Shearith Israel, New York City

PARTICIPANTS

Dr. Norman Lamm, Yeshiva University
Rabbi Marc D. Angel, Spanish-Portuguese Synagogue, New York
Prof. David Berger, Brooklyn College and Yeshiva University
Rabbi Saul Berman, Yeshiva University
Rabbi Louis Bernstein, Yeshiva University
Dr. Moshe Bernstein, Yeshiva University
Rabbi Yoel Bin-Nun, Yeshivat Har Etzion
Dr. Rivkah Blau, Shevach High School for Women
Rabbi Yosef Blau, RIETS/Yeshiva University
Dr. Judith Bleich, Touro College
Dr. Jay Braverman, Yeshiva of Flatbush
Rabbi Shalom Carmy, Yeshiva University
Rabbi Zevulun Charlop, RIETS/Yeshiva University
Dr. Carol Diament, Hadassah
Prof. Eliezer Don-Yehiya, Bar-Ilan University
Mr. Daniel Ehrlich, RIETS/Yeshiva University
Dr. Yaakov Elman, Yeshiva University
Prof. Aharon Enker, Bar-Ilan University
Rabbi Emanuel Feldman, Congregation Beth Jacob, Atlanta, GA
Rabbi Meir Goldwicht, Yeshiva University

Dr. Lawrence Grossman, American Jewish Committee
Rabbi Nathaniel Helfgot, Frisch Yeshiva High School
Rabbi Robert S. Hirt, RIETS/Yeshiva University
Dr. Ephraim Kanarfogel, RIETS/Yeshiva University
Dr. Lawrence Kaplan, McGill University
Rabbi Aharon Lichtenstein, Yeshivat Har Etzion/Gruss Institute, RIETS
Dr. Israel Miller, Yeshiva University
Rabbi Yaakov Neuburger, RIETS/Yeshiva University
Rabbi Michael Rosensweig, RIETS/Yeshiva University
Rabbi Sol Roth, Yeshiva University and Fifth Avenue Synagogue,
    New York
Rabbi Yonason Sacks, Yeshiva University High Schools
Dr. Jacob J. Schacter, The Jewish Center, New York
Dr. Alvin Schiff, Board of Jewish Education, New York
Dr. David Shatz, Yeshiva University
Dr. Moshe Sokol, Touro College
Rabbi Moshe D. Tendler, RIETS/Yeshiva University
Dr. Chaim I. Waxman, Rutgers University and Yeshiva University
Dr. Joel Wolowelsky, Yeshiva of Flatbush High School
Rabbi Walter S. Wurzburger, Yeshiva University and Congregation
    Shaarey Tefilah, Long Island

לז"נ מורי חותני

הרה"ג ר' דוד בהר"ר יעקב אריה, זצ"ל

אב"ד דק"ק סובלק, וכיובל שנים
ר"מ בישיבת רבנו יצחק אלחנן:

עבד את ה' ופעל עבור הכלל והפרט,
התורה, העם, והארץ
בכל לבבו, בכל נפשו, ובכל מאודו:

נקרא לישיבה של מעלה ט' תמוז תשנ"ג
תנצב"ה

Contents

Preface

Chaim I. Waxman

Although outsiders frequently assume that Orthodox Jewry is mono-lithic, it is, actually, a rather heterogeneous group. Indeed, as Eliezer Don-Yehiya convincingly demonstrates in his article in this volume, place does matter. This can also be seen in the differing stances of American and Eastern European Orthodoxy toward Zionism in the early twentieth century.

In contrast to Eastern European Orthodoxy, which was charac-terized in the prestate era by its anti-Zionism, American Orthodoxy was always highly supportive of the establishment of the Jewish state. Mizrachi, the religious Zionist movement, was one of the major forces in American Orthodoxy, more influential by far than the non-Zionist Agudath Israel.[1] During the interwar period, Yeshiva Torah

---

[1]Menahem Kaufman, *Lo-Ziyonim be-America be-Maavak al ha-Medinah, 1939–1948* (Jerusalem: Zionist Library, World Zionist Organization, 1984), 7. For a historical overview, albeit somewhat romanticized, of the Mizrachi in

Veda'ath, one of the first higher *yeshivahs* in the United States, was strongly Zionist.[2] As recently as 1949, *Hapardes* (the oldest extant Torah journal in the United States) contained regular reports on religious Zionist developments, both within Mizrachi and beyond it. Among the features in the April 1949 issue, for example, is a detailed report on an address delivered by Rabbi David Lifshitz to the annual convention of the Union of Orthodox Rabbis of the United States and Canada ("*Agudat HaRabbanim*"), in which strong sentiments of religious Zionism are expressed.[3]

Today, much of that picture has changed dramatically. American Orthodox Judaism is now heavily influenced by Agudath Israel. Religious Zionism, if it is not loudly condemned, is rarely mentioned in the aforementioned Torah journal; the leadership of *Agudat HaRabbanim* is wholly of the Agudath Israel persuasion; and the "*yeshivishe velt*," the "world of the *yeshivah*," is virtually synonymous with the world of non-Zionism. This is a result, in large measure, of the post–Second World War immigration to America of the survivors of Eastern European Orthodoxy—including those of the scholarly elite who headed the higher *yeshivot* in Russia, Lithuania, and Poland—as well as a number hasidic grand rabbis and their followers, most of whom came from Hungary, Czechoslovakia, and Poland.[4] Establishing a network of day schools and *yeshivahs* in America that socialized a

---

the United States, see Aaron Halevi Pachenik, "Ha-Ziyonut ha-Datit be-Arzot ha-Berit," in *Sefer ha-Ziyonut ha-Datit*, ed. Yitzchak Raphael and S. Z. Shragai (Jerusalem: Mossad HaRav Kook, 1977), 2:226–41.

[2]Jenna Weissman Joselit, *New York's Jewish Jews: The Orthodox Community in the Interwar Years* (Bloomington, IN: Indiana University Press, 1990), 17.

[3]*Hapardes* 23:7 (April 1949): 12–15. See also p. 10, which contains a report of the New York visit of Rabbi Yoseph Kahanman, "one of the great heads of yeshivahs, of Ponivezh, and now of the state of Israel." The last phrase in Hebrew is "*Medinat Yisrael*," not "*Eretz Yisrael*."

[4]Somewhat surprisingly, there is still no thorough study of American Orthodoxy, especially since World War II. For some thoughts on what such a study should encompass, see Charles S. Liebman, "Studying Ortho-

new generation in accordance with their non-Zionist version of Orthodoxy, these new arrivals soon took over the ideological leadership of the Agudath Israel of America and provided it with a following from within the rank and file of *yeshivah* students and *hasidim*. By the 1950s, Agudath Israel had grown to be one of the largest and most influential organizations of American Orthodoxy, whereas Mizrachi's leadership had stagnated, and its membership and significance had declined markedly.

Not only within "the world of the *yeshivah*,"[5] but within much of American Orthodoxy in general, the ideology of religious Zionism is now much less frequently espoused. Indeed, when ArtScroll Publishers, a highly successful publisher of traditional Judaica that caters to the Orthodox public, put out a new edition of the traditional prayer book, it omitted the prayer for the welfare of the state of Israel.

---

dox Judaism in the United States: A Review Essay," *American Jewish History* 80:3 (Spring 1991): 415–24.

[5] William B. Helmreich, *The World of the Yeshiva* (New York: Free Press, 1983). This is the "world" known as the *haredi*, "black-hat," "right-wing," or "ultra-Orthodox" community. Helmreich includes Yeshiva University's Rabbi Isaac Elchanan Theological Seminary (RIETS) in his analysis. However, RIETS is clearly peripheral to the world of the *yeshivah* and not considered as part of it by the overwhelming majority of that world. As he suggests, it "is viewed by many in the other major yeshivahs as not being part of the community because it not only permits secular education but maintains a college on its campus that is a required part of study for all undergraduates" (p. 36). Although Helmreich makes no mention of it, there is every reason to suggest that the religious Zionism espoused in RIETS only confirms its "deviant" status. On the growing influence of the *haredi* perspective within Orthodoxy, see Menachem Friedman, "Life Tradition and Book Tradition in the Development of Ultraorthodox Judaism," in *Judaism Viewed from Within and From Without: Anthropological Perspectives*, ed. Harvey E. Goldberg (Albany: State University of New York Press, 1987), 235–55; Chaim I. Waxman, "Toward a Sociology of *Pesak*," *Rabbinic Authority and Personal Autonomy*, ed. Moshe Z. Sokol (Northvale, NJ: Jason Aronson, 1992), 217–37.

Although the organization of modern Orthodox rabbis, the Rabbinical Council of America, issued its own special edition of the
ArtScroll *siddur* that included this prayer, it appears that the regular
edition has become the standard one for the Orthodox public in the
United States.[6] Likewise, there seems to have been a decline in the
religious celebration of Israel Independence Day within Orthodox
congregations across the United States.

Such developments, however, do not indicate a decline in support for Israel within American Orthodoxy. Quite the contrary. As
I have analyzed elsewhere,[7] a series of surveys conducted during the
1980s indicated that the extent of Orthodox Jews' attachments to
Israel—however measured—greatly exceeds those among other de-
nominations, and these patterns prevail among American Jewish
institutional leaders as well as the community at large. Not only are
American Orthodox Jews more knowledgeable about and more personally involved with Israel than are other American Jews, their per-

---

[6]It is perhaps even more revealing that ArtScroll Publishers blatantly
omitted a phrase implying religious Zionist sentiments from its translation
of Rabbi S. Y. Zevin's *Ha-Mo'adim be-Halakhah*. See Reuven P. Bulka,
"Israel and the State of the Religious Mind," *Morasha: A Journal of Religious
Zionism* 2:2 (Spring-Summer 1986): 30–34. For another critique of the
ArtScroll phenomenon, see B. Barry Levy, "Judge Not a Book by Its
Cover," *Tradition* 19:1 (Spring 1981): 89–95, and the response by Emanuel
Feldman, *Tradition* 19:2 (Summer 1981): 192. For a more extensive version
of Levy's critique, see his article, "Our Torah, Your Torah and Their To-
rah: An Evaluation of the ArtScroll Phenomenon," in *Truth and Compas-
sion: Essays on Judaism and Religion in Memory of Rabbi Dr. Solomon Frank*,
ed. Howard Joseph, Jack N. Lightstone, and Michael D. Oppenheim (Wa-
terloo, Ontario: Canadian Corporation for Studies in Religion/Wilfrid
Laurier University Press, 1983), 137–89.

[7]Chaim I. Waxman, "All In the Family: American Jewish Attachments
to Israel," in *A New Jewry?: America Since the Second World War*, Studies
in Contemporary Jewry, vol. 8, ed. Peter Y. Medding (New York, Oxford
University Press, 1992), 134–49.

sonal involvements became markedly deeper and stronger from the mid-1970s through the mid-1980s. These patterns were reconfirmed in the 1990 National Jewish Population Survey.[8]

Nevertheless, there seems to have been a *transformation* in the role of Israel within American Orthodoxy, although its precise nature is not yet quite clear. It may be that there is a decline in the tendency to define the State of Israel within the context of modern (albeit religious) Zionism and an increasing tendency to define Israel traditionally, as *Eretz Yisrael*—a trend that has also manifested itself within Israel, especially since the Begin era.[9] Alternatively, the transformation may be characterized as the secularization of Israel. Perhaps because Israel has become so modernized, American Orthodox Jews increasingly relate to it as a modern secular society to which, nevertheless, strong allegiances are attached because it is a state in which Jews are sovereign.[10]

In all, religious Zionist ideology that defines Israel in religious terms has lost influence, so much so that today most American Orthodox Jews no longer overtly conceive of Israel in ritualistic-religious terms. They remain strongly attached to Israel as the state of the Jewish people and therefore deserving of high communal priority, but the state per se is not part of the specifically religious

---

[8]Chaim I. Waxman, *Jewish Baby Boomers* (Albany: State University of New York Press, in press).

[9]Cf. Charles S. Liebman and Eliezer Don-Yehiya, *Civil Religion in Israel: Traditional Judaism and Political Culture in the Jewish State* (Berkeley: University of California Press, 1983), 123–66.

[10]Such an approach is somewhat similar to the religious Zionism espoused by Rabbi Jacob Reines, rather than to that of Rabbi Abraham Isaac Kook. See Michael Zvi Nehorai, "Rav Reines and Rav Kook: Two Approaches to Zionism," in *The World of Rav Kook's Thought* (New York: Avi Chai, 1991), 255–67. This book is a translation, by Shalom Carmy and Bernard Casper, of *Yovel Orot: Haguto shel ha-Rav Avraham Yitzhak ha-Cohen Kook*, ed. Binyamin Ish Shalom and Shalom Rosenberg (Jerusalem: World Zionist Organization, Torah Education Department, 1985).

realm.[11] In any event, even the sectarian Orthodox can now openly express their attachments to *Eretz Yisrael* and the people of Israel without being tainted by secular Zionism.

The organizers of and participants in the Third Orthodox Forum (in which the articles in this book were initially presented), however, perceive the State of Israel as a religious reality having halakhic significance for all of Judaism and Jewry. As Yoel Bin-Nun explicitly avers, and as is implicit in almost all of the articles in this volume, the establishment of the sovereign Jewish state is halakhically revolutionary and creates a set of real, rather than merely hypothetical, relationships and obligations between world Jewry and the State of

---

[11]For evidence that there is a correlation between religiosity and national Jewish identity and identification, see Simon N. Herman, *Israelis and Jews: The Continuity of an Identity* (New York: Random House, 1970); John E. Hofman, "Ha-Zehut ha-Yehudit shel No'ar Yehudi be-Yisrael," *Megamot* 17:1 (January 1970): 5–14; Rina Shapira and Eva Etzioni-Halevy, *Mi Atah HaStudent HaIsraeli* (Tel Aviv: 1973); a series of surveys conducted in Israel in 1974 by Shlomit Levy and Louis E. Guttman and published in Jerusalem during that year in four parts by Israel Institute of Applied Social Research (Part IV, *Values and Attitudes of Israeli High School Youth*, contains an English summary); Eva Etzioni-Halevy and Rina Shapira, "Jewish Identification of Israeli Students: What Lies Ahead," *Jewish Social Studies* 37:3–4 (July-October 1975): 251–66; Simon N. Herman, *Jewish Identity: A Social Psychological Perspective*, 2nd ed. (New Brunswick, NJ: Transaction Books, 1989); Eva Etzioni-Halevy and Rina Shapira, *Political Culture in Israel: Cleavage and Integration Among Israeli Jews* (New York: Praeger, 1977), 157–78.

A recent incident that I personally witnessed reiterated to me the validity of the above assertion. A group of several hundred religiously observant Jews, overwhelmingly modern Orthodox, were together at a hotel for Pesach. When, after several days, the leader of the prayer services was asked why there was no recitation of the prayer for the welfare of the State of Israel (*Tefillah lishlom ha-medinah*), he replied: "We don't have any time for it; we have to be finished at. . . ." That individual

Israel. In addition, the fact that Israel will probably be the home of the majority of world Jewry within the foreseeable future gives it even more halakhic significance and means that two of the three criteria suggested by Rambam (Maimonides) for the Messianic era will have been realized.

The conference papers upon which the essays in this volume are based inspired much thought and valuable discussion. It is hoped that in their revised form for this volume they will reach an even wider audience and help stimulate new religious Zionist thought and action in the American Orthodox community as well as those worldwide.

It is an honor and pleasure to publicly thank Dr. Norman Lamm, president of Yeshiva University, for having both created the Orthodox Forum and for taking such an active role in all of its deliberations. Rabbi Robert S. Hirt, vice president for Administration and Professional Education of the Rabbi Isaac Elchanan Theological Seminary, an affiliate of Yeshiva University, is a long-time friend and the individual most deeply involved in all of the details of the Orthodox Forum, and I hope he knows how much his devotion, efforts, and wise counsel are appreciated. Daniel Ehrlich was the staff person assigned to provide technical assistance to the forum, which he did admirably with both professionalism and personal commitment. To my colleagues on the steering committee I owe appreciation not only for bestowing upon me the privilege of organizing and chairing the third Orthodox Forum, but also for working with me as a team to make it as meaningful as it was.

In addition to the efforts of the conference sponsors, organizers, and participants, I gratefully acknowledge the assistance and translation skills of Rabbi Chaim Bronstein and Yosef Cohen and the technical assistance of Aaron Dobin.

---

and, indeed, virtually everyone present were highly supportive of Israel but simply did not relate to it religiously and, thus, felt no religious need to include a special prayer for its welfare.

I also appreciate the dedication as well as the editorial and publication skills of Arthur Kurzweil, Muriel Jorgensen, Jean Pease, and the staff of Jason Aronson Inc. They helped transform a group of papers into a beautifully published volume.

1

A View from the Fleshpots: Exploratory Remarks on Gilded Galut Existence

Shalom Carmy

Redemption involves a movement by an individual or a community from the periphery of history to its center; or, to employ a term from physics, redemption is a centripetal movement. To be on the periphery means to be a non–history-making entity, while movement toward the center renders the same entity history-making and history-conscious.

—Rabbi Joseph B. Soloveitchik[1]

It happens that moral awareness advances more than free moral capacity. Then adding knowledge adds many pains, for one sees with open eye, how his own moral rifts torment his soul, and he walks gloomily under the pressure of his own depressed will, because of the provocation of the moral capacity, that has not yet developed to the level of awareness. But these sufferings are sufferings of love; at last they bring complete light. . . . The entire environment, external and objective, also helps to actualize the capacity concealed in the power of awareness. For the movement to elevate

[1]"Redemption, Prayer, Talmud Torah," *Tradition* 17:2 (Spring 1978): 55.

*being is not enclosed in any specific substance in itself; the movement
expands and spreads through all the pertinent circumference.*

—Rabbi Abraham I. Kook[2]

*The promised land guarantees nothing. It is only an opportunity, not a deliv-
erance.*

—Shelby Steele[3]

That there is, and must be, a qualitative difference between Jewish
existence and religious experience in Israel and that of *Galut* is more
obvious for most of us than the precise character of that difference.
When we attempt to define the difference we tend to veer off in one
of two directions. With soaring spirit, we sing the poetry of the Land
of Israel, dreaming awake the eschatological word, seeking in the
quotidian only its inverted root in the transcendent, waxing metaphysical in the wonderful Kookian world. A series of binary contrasts
then yields the philosophical concept of *Galut*. The limitation of this
vision, for our purposes, is twofold: It describes the world, not as we
ordinarily experience it but as we should like to experience it; moreover, in turning its gaze upon *Eretz Yisrael*, it can only see *Galut* as a
shadowy negative of Israel's reality.

The earth-bound alternative is to catalog the differences as we
discover them: the price, quality, and availability of vegetables; the
rates of burglary in Ramat Gan and Teaneck; the state of *yeshivot*; the
headaches of *shemittah* (the Sabbatical year) versus the burdens of
Yom Tov sheni (the extra day observed in the Diaspora); soccer versus
baseball. Whether this work is prosecuted analytically and compre-
hensively by social scientists or, as most people prefer, with relaxed
anecdotal particularity, the difficulty, for our purpose, is that such
discussion fails to distinguish America as *Galut* from Israel as *Eretz
Yisrael*; one might as well be sizing up the merits of Boston and
Omaha. It is not surprising that this approach, combusted with the

---

[2] *Orot haKodesh* 3, no. 62.

[3] *The Content of Our Characters* (New York: St. Martin's Press, 1990),
175.

precipitate of cynicism that is the underside of the first, is sometimes compatible with a third position: namely, that contemporary religious life is essentially the same in Israel and in America.

In what follows I hope to steer clear of these alternatives. Instead, I will try to focus on the way religious Jews (more specifically, religious Zionists), living in the United States, experience their life in *Galut*.[4] The characteristics on which my discussion will focus are not accidental attributes of American life but inherent properties of the *Galut* situation in the West.

Let me also distinguish our inquiry from two distinct, though related, subjects. The question of halakhic obligations connected with life in Israel and America surely ought to affect our lives but is not identical with that of how we experience our lives. By the same token, the theology of *Galut*, by which I mean all the religiously interesting propositions about *Galut* (for example, why the present one has been prolonged, what we can infer from it about the workings of Providence), may have implications for the experience of contemporary American Jews but does not uniquely define it. One need not live in *Galut* to have a correct theological perspective on it; leaving *Galut* may well be an advantage.

The first sections of our discussion deal with the manner in which the religious Zionist might account for his or her existence in *Galut*, first as an individual, then as a component of a significant part of the Jewish people. We will then engage the present situation confronting the Orthodox world. Finally, we shall comment on the implications of our analysis and the problems it leaves outstanding.

I

No discussion of the individual in *Galut* under contemporary (non–Rabbi Hayyim HaKohen)[5] conditions can avoid confronting the

---

[4]Arnold Eisen, *Galut* (Bloomington, IN: Indiana University Press, 1986), presents perspectives on the place of Exile in Jewish thought that are stimulating and often original. The absence of correlation between his

halakhic desirability of *aliyah*. All things being equal, it is better that a God-fearing Jew live in the Land of Israel than outside it. Ramban's opinion that there is a specific commandment to settle the Land is only one factor in this judgment. To it one may add the opportunity to fulfill the commandments dependent upon the Land,[6] and the spiritual benefit that the Holy Land bestows upon its inhabitants.[7] It is posited that in Israel, when the Jewish people dwell in the Land, practical occupations have a religious value that is absent in Exile.[8] Moreover, if "[t]he Jew who identifies with his people [is one who] wishes to be at the cutting edge of its history—. . . that, today is in Israel."[9]

---

treatment and mine is due to differences of theological orientation and normative commitment. Among studies that reached me too late to incorporate in the text, I must mention several of the essays in *Eretz Yisrael be-Hagut ha-Yehudit be-Yemei ha-Benayim*, ed. M. Hallamish and A. Ravitzky (Jerusalem: Yad Izhak Ben-Zvi, 1991), and Eliezer Don-Yehiya, ed., *Israel and Diaspora Jewry: Ideological and Political Perspectives* (Ramat Gan: Bar-Ilan University Press, 1991), particularly the articles by Immanuel Jakobovitz, Jonathan Sacks, Chaim I. Waxman, Daniel Gutenmacher, and Eliezer Don-Yehiya. Also see Todd Endelman, "The Legitimation of the Diaspora Experience in Recent Jewish Historiography," *Modern Judaism* 11:2 (May, 1991): 195–210. An unpublished paper by Zvi Grumet, "The Extent of (Religious) Zionist Education in the Modern Orthodox Yeshiva High School," written for a course in Yeshiva University's Azrieli Graduate Institute for Jewish Education and Administration (Summer 1992), surveys the sociological literature on the subject.

[5]*Tosafot Ketubbot* 110b, s.v. *ve-Hi omeret*.

[6]See *Sotah* 14a.

[7]For a halakhic survey see Hershel Schachter, "The Mitzvah of Yishuv Eretz Yisrael," in *Religious Zionism*, ed. Shubert Spero and Yitzchak Pessin (Jerusalem: Mesilot and World Zionist Organization, 1989), 190–212. The issue of Special Providence is discussed in several of the contributions in *Eretz Yisrael be-Hagut ha-Yehudit*, ed. M. Hallamish and A. Ravitzky.

[8]*Hatam Sofer* to *Lulav ha-Gazul* 36a, s.v. *Domeh*.

[9]Gerald J. Blidstein, "American Jews and Israel," *Tradition* 18:1 (Summer 1979): 11.

From an experiential point of view, the most clear-cut token of halakhic commitment to living in Israel is the petition we recite thrice daily: "May our eyes behold Your return to Zion with mercy." Centuries ago the king of the Kuzari observed that, absent genuine intention to live in Israel, our gestures and protestations are either hypocrisy or rote.[10] Jewish belief and practice thus presuppose the desire to live in Israel, at the very least as a higher-order desire.[11]

At the same time, it is a fact that the vast majority of observant Jews, be they laymen, local leaders, or even major rabbinic personalities, do not regard living in Israel as a perfect, ineluctable duty, like hearing the shofar, devoting minimal time to Torah, or even snacking in the *sukkah*. There are hard-liners who insist on the absolute obligation to dwell in Israel, and those who remain in America are presumably hard-pressed to explain the inconsistency. They must also, wherever they live, account for the failure of paradigmatic figures—Rabbi Moshe Feinstein and *maran ha-Rav* Joseph B. Soloveitchik being two conspicuous examples—to promote vigorously the approved axiology. Most of us, at a practical level, endorse *aliyah*, from a halakhic vantage point, while treating it as an optional value, the omission of which is no dereliction of religious duty. Some make of where to live a serious matter, a bit like the choice of profession or spouse, a significant, though not obligatory, life-shaping act. For the more hardheaded it is more like an exotic, honored-in-the-breach *humrah*: encountered sporadically only to be straightaway dismissed from consciousness.

Not choosing *aliyah* is thus sociologically valid for the bulk of the religious Zionist community of North America. In many cases it can also be defended halakhically, with varying degrees of justification. Available reasons range over a broad spectrum. A rabbi, for example, comes to consider the work on which he is engaged as so

---

[10]*Kuzari* II, 23–24.

[11]For the distinction between orders of desire and its application to the akratic problem, see H. Frankfurt, "Freedom of the Will and the Concept of the Person," *Journal of Philosophy* 68 (January 1971): 5–20.

vital that it supersedes other commitments. And there are other exemptions. As Rabbi Schachter puts it, expounding the view of the *Avnei Nezer*: "There is no mitzvah of *yishuv ha-Aretz* ... unless one will have a *klitah tovah*—a successful absorption process."[12] Acknowledging that one has not had, or is unlikely to have, a *klitah tovah*, is rather unflattering, whether one is a yuppie forced to confess himself too dependent on creature comforts to contemplate a change of place, a ne'er-do-well, unable to hold one's own in the Israeli job market, or a hypertensive who cannot cope with the bureaucracy. Quite often, I suspect, the reasons for remaining in *Galut* are more muddled than ideologists assume.

My interest here is not in adjudicating the correctness of individual justifications for failure to live in Israel. It is rather in the consequences of such attempts at self-justification for the spiritual life. The most direct consequence of the need to justify living in America is that one devotes attention to that justification; where Zionist consciousness is high, the justification often occurs in the presence of others.

How one judges such self-justification depends, to a large extent, on the evaluation of self-justification in general. *Heshbon ha-nefesh* (self-examination) is an integral part of ethical existence, universally extolled by *baalei musar* (moralists). Going to school to anxiety, standing at the crossroads before the great choices of life, is thus an education toward the "examined life," the life that is worth living. Whatever precipitates self-examination is good, and if thought about where one lives leads to self-examination, then that is good, too. At the same time, chronic self-justification, especially when it takes place in public, is likely to harden into rehearsed complacency, on the one hand, or aimless guilt feelings, on the other hand. The public focus may skew our understanding of the reasons for our choices. We acknowledge the attraction of material goals and decry inertial forces, we emphasize the value of our contributions to American Jewish life, while tending to underestimate the pull of family obligations

---

[12]Hershel Schachter, "The Mitzvah of Yishuv Eretz Yisrael," 210 n. 39.

and comforts, of the small local and professional duties and pleasures that make up so much of the meaning and structure of our lives.

The depth of our soul-searching may also be open to question. Take, for example, a prominent scholar-thinker who digresses from his remarks on Rabbi Levi Yitzhak of Berditchev to articulate these feelings: "I regret my life in the exile. . . . We must live there [in Israel], or at least yearn to live there and feel guilty and unfulfilled if we do not."[13] One may agree with the judgment without grasping its message to us as individuals. Guilt, like other categories of inwardness, corresponds to a range of slippery, shifting experiences. Are we dealing with what recent philosophers call "rational regret,"[14] that is, a regret that does not imply a change of mind on the part of the agent? If so, what makes the regret rational? Is it, instead, the guilt of the akratic (weak of will) individual, or that of wrong reasoners who would mend their ways? In any case, is feeling guilty a sufficient earnest of penitence; should not *yearning* to live in Israel make way for *planning* to live there?

Untempered suspicion toward those who feel guilty about their failure to live in Israel (or their failure to yearn and plan steadily for that eventuality) constitutes uncalled-for cynicism. Yet a constant self-conscious dwelling upon that failure suggests a measure of accommodation with moral haplessness. Such a preoccupation reverberates with a melancholy alienation from one's determinate identity and the wistful idealization of low-grade *schlemielkeit* as an acceptable relation to the world of action. This psychological (cultural, spiritual?) homelessness, in turn, is regarded as characteristic of a certain type of rootless Jewish sophisticate, memorably enacted by the early persona of Woody Allen. Here the sense of guilt is stripped of its deontological qualities, as it were, and transformed into an ironic detachment from ethical existence, a guilt whose ultimate aim is

---

[13]David Blumenthal, *God at the Center* (New York: Harper & Row, 1988), 138.

[14]For example, S. L. Hurley, *Natural Reasons* (New York: Oxford University Press, 1989), 171ff.

to be troubled only by the confirmed habit of continuing to feel guilty.

The sense of determinate meaning inseparable from Orthodox belief and practice renders our community in America less indulgent of such an attitude to guilt than less committed Jews. Moreover, because we tend to identify this personality type with assimilation, we are, as a rule, critical of its manifestations. Nonetheless, it can be argued, the temptation to wallow ineffectually in the feeling of regret and guilt is inherent in our very situation: insisting, on the one hand, that it is wrong for us to remain in America, that our lives are radically unfulfilled, yet not doing very much to change things. Thus the concern with self-justification that accompanies the American Zionist, and especially the religious one, is a double-edged sword. What is gained in self-examination may be lost through indulgence in unproductive self-laceration and self-reification.

Religious Israeli Jews are presumably exempt from the need to justify their place of residence. They are, after all, where they are supposed to be and must mine their quota of angst from other quarries. This triggers a complaint sometimes heard in non-Zionist Orthodox circles: that the Israeli Zionist considers himself superior to other Jews by virtue of being in Israel and, hence, smugly deems himself beyond traditional soul-searching. Whatever the pertinence of this allegation to the lives of Jews in Israel, it deserves attention as an expression of the feelings of Jews in exile. Is it merely reflective of the attitudes of critics who would cut religious Zionism down to size, or does it also say something about American Zionists who hope that *Eretz Yisrael* will resolve for them inadequacies that seem intractable in their present surroundings?

II

So far we have looked at American religious Zionists as individuals coming to terms with their abode. The individual may, however, interpret his or her existence as part of the historical fate and destiny of the Jewish people as a whole. Note, however, that in one salient respect the analysis of the collective is not analogous to that of the individual. When the individual justifies, on whatever grounds, his living in America, he has put to rest, at least temporarily, the question that required justification. To explain what functions the Jewish people (or a large segment of the Jewish people) must (or may) fulfill in *Galut* justifies the nation (or a large portion of the nation) remaining in *Galut*. Whether a particular individual ought to be one of the *Galut*-dwellers is an additional question, requiring further deliberation on the part of the individual. With this caveat in mind, we shall examine several theories according to which the Jewish people in exile is to accomplish worthwhile, perhaps even necessary, tasks in the divine economy.

LIGHT TO THE NATIONS

We are accustomed to dismiss the notion that Israel is dispersed among the nations in order to bring them the kerygma of Judaism as the dated relic of an age hungry for emancipation, drunk on the dogma of universal progress. A reminder is in order that Rabbi Bahye b. Asher, a writer whose eclectic taste surely did not extend to the anticipatory appreciation of nineteenth-century fashions, placed it first among the reasons for the Dispersion: "That Israel should spread among the unintelligent nations, that those nations learn from them belief in the existence of God and the flow of Providence regarding the particulars of men."[15] Its most powerful literary expression, the parable of the Jewish people as a seed buried in the earth, invisibly generating the spiritual movements that bring mankind closer to God, was written by Rabbi Yehudah Halevi, in a book distinguished

---

[15]*Kad ha-Kemah* in *Kitve Rabbenu Bahye* (ed. Chavel, Jerusalem 5730) 114f. (cf. Maharsha, *Pesahim* 87b s.v. *lo hegla*). That this discussion of exile occurs in the section called *Ge'ullah* illustrates the tendency of Jewish thinkers to treat *Galut* as a negative concept, the hiatus between normal stages of existence. See also Shalom Rosenberg, "Exile to Israel in 16th Century Jewish Thought," in *Eretz Yisrael be-Hagut ha-Yehudit*, 174–81.

for its commendation of *aliyah*.[16] The mission of Israel is not the
brainchild of German Reform; it is an old and respectable conception
for Jewish thought.

Nevertheless, in modern times, this idea speaks with a German
accent. Within the Torah world it is stamped with the personality of
Rabbi Samson Raphael Hirsch. Early in his career, Hirsch already
envisioned the emancipated ideal Jew

> dwelling in freedom in the midst of the nations, and striving to
> attain unto its ideal, every son of Israel a respected and influ-
> ential exemplar priest of righteousness and love, disseminating
> among the nations not specific Judaism, for proselytism is inter-
> dicted, but pure humanity.[17]

The following two assumptions underlie this passage:

1. The conditions of *Galut* permit, and even promote, a dignified and inspiring Jewish existence. Beneath the encrusted distor-
tions and compulsions of the past, glimmer the opportunities of civil-
ity and free religious practice.

2. Fulfillment of the first assumption contributes to the substantial spiritual improvement of our Gentile neighbors.

Both assumptions are open to question. They are often rejected
because the brave new world of European Jewry turned ugly. From its
inception, the Zionist outlook held that subjugation and persecution
degraded the Jew's spirit, inevitably undercutting his ability to instruct the world.[18] To be sure, the degraded Job of the nineteenth
century had not completely lost the capacity to teach, even to inspire,
though he cannot offer himself as a "respected and influential exem-

---

[16]*Kuzari* 4:23.

[17]*Nineteen Letters*, trans. B. Drachman (New York: Feldheim, 1942),
Letter 16, 163.

[18]For a theological exposition of this critique, see Netziv, *Rinnah shel
Torah* (Warsaw, 5694) 96 (to *Shir ha-Shirim* 7:1).

plar" of dignified existence; the murdered Job of our century cannot do that either. In the absence of minimal physical security the Jew cannot teach, and the Gentile cannot benefit from his lesson. This critique, however, loses sight of the conviction that "America is different," if not forever, at least for the time being.[19] And it is today in which we live.

The contemporary American neo-Hirschian is vulnerable to a different question: What precisely is the "pure humanity" that the Jew is to disseminate? Assuming that it is in our power to bring that message to others, how is it to be communicated? Hirsch seems to hold, quite reasonably, that the message is to be disseminated by personal example. Personal example of what? Human beings who exemplify virtue are scarce in any age, not least in our secular wasteland. Yet honesty, fidelity, modesty, conscience, courage, altruism, love are not unknown in the gentile world past and present. That these qualities have survived and sometimes even prospered is largely due to the insertion of the Jewish people into history; even more so has the story of God and the Jews testified to His concern for the destiny of man. But this does not entail that we Jews can best contribute to the flourishing of virtue by dwelling among the Gentiles or by maximizing our intercourse with them.

If we Jews, in our time, are called upon to establish a model of human dignity and to make a place for God in history, it might well be presumed that our arena of striving and teaching should coincide with the area that is both essential to the modern world and in which Gentile resources have failed most spectacularly. "In our times," wrote Thomas Mann of our age, long before its deepest horrors came to light, "the destiny of man presents its meaning in political terms."[20] Subsequent history has demonstrated only too patently man's fallibility in the face of that destiny. Far from separating the

---

[19]The subjugation of the Jew also carries with it an element of *hillul ha-Shem* separate from any debasement of the Jewish character (see, for example, Ezekiel 36:20ff.).

[20]Epigraph to William Butler Yeats, "Politics."

Jewish people from its teaching vocation, the Zionist project, from this point of view, submits us to the exemplary challenge of contemporary existence.[21] An eminent Israeli scientist speaks for many when he writes:

> In returning to Zion, we have put ourselves and Judaism irrevocably on the line. . . . We lived the epoch of galut in self-knowledge of a very real question: are our brave value affirmations for real, or are they in the modern world largely a privilege of weakness?[22]

Rabbi Kook articulates this mode of analysis when he claims that it is our destiny in exile that reflects the obscure, introverted, self-cultivating, *emet ve-emunah*, pole of Jewish existence, while our lives in Israel manifest the extroverted, daylight, *emet ve-yatziv*, pole.[23] When we consider where the Jew can best serve as example and inspiration to the nations, the problem with Israel is not that it is an evasion of the challenge, but, on the contrary, that it is all too real. Besides, setting a moral example while living with Arabs in Israel is no less a task than inspiring an audience of Polish charwomen or black token clerks in Brooklyn.

---

[21]Isadore Twersky has suggested that Rabbi Yehudah Halevi and Maimonides disagreed on this point, with the former maintaining that the "mission of Israel" can only be fulfilled through exile. See I. Twersky, "Maimonides on Eretz Yisrael: Halakhic, Philosophic and Historical Perspectives," in *Perspectives on Maimonides: Philosophical and Historical Studies*, ed. Joel Kraemer (New York: Oxford University Press, 1991), 257–90, 284 n. 40.

[22]David W. Weiss, "A Value Dependence on the Diaspora," *Tradition* 22:2 (Summer 1986): 41.

[23]*Ein Ayyah* to *Berakhot*, no. 1 (Jerusalem, 5749). Rabbi Kook is expounding on the difference between the phrases with which the benedictions immediately following the *Shema* commence in the morning and evening liturgy, with morning corresponding to life in Israel and evening symbolizing *Galut* existence.

The neo-Hirschian may counter this pro-*aliyah* version of the "light unto the nations" position in two ways. He may concede that Israel offers greater opportunities for exemplary living but insist that we are enjoined, for whatever reasons, from taking advantage of these opportunities by returning to Israel at this time. This view is, by definition, outside the pale of religious Zionism and, hence, need not detain us here.

Alternatively, one might tolerate living in *Galut*, under certain circumstances, as a *be-di'avad*. The desire to instruct and inspire the nations is not, ordinarily, a sufficient reason for remaining in North America. Individual Jews, however, finding themselves in *Galut* for a variety of reasons, are to make the best of their fate by undertaking the Hirschian vocation. From this point of view, inspiring Gentiles will not, by itself, all things being equal, serve to justify life in *Galut*; it can, however, make that life more worthwhile and purposeful.

VENTILATION VARIATION

There is another aspect of Hirsch's conception that we may best appreciate by catching a glimpse of him in a moment of exegesis. The problem is Abraham's seemingly unmotivated journey to Gerar shortly before the birth of Isaac. Hirsch ventures the following:

> An Isaac should grow up again in isolation, away from every pernicious influence. But complete isolation where the youth never comes into contact with other people, other thoughts, people living different lives and aims, is an equally dangerous fault in education. A young man who has never seen any other way of life than that of his parents, who has never learnt to value, respect, and hold fast to that life by its moral contrast to others, surely falls readily under these strange influences as soon as he meets them, just as the anxious shutting out of all fresh air is the surest way of catching cold the first time one goes out. The son of Abraham, the future continuer of the heritage of Abraham is, from time to time, to go into the non-

Abrahamitic world, there to learn to estimate what is in opposition to it, and to steel himself by practice, in the midst of a
world opposed to the spirit and way of life of Abraham, to keep
himself faithful and true to his mission. For that purpose
Abraham chose the residential city of a Philistine prince. In the
land of the Philistines the degeneration seems not to have
reached the depth of their Amorite neighbours, and therefore
they had not been included in the destruction.[24]

While Hirsch stresses here the "mission of Abraham," he is also concerned about the development of Isaac, who, unless immunized
through exposure to the world, is in danger of falling under its sway.
If confrontation with an alien world is inevitable, then education to
the knowledge of the world is desirable, quite apart from our ability
to influence others; and if knowledge by acquaintance is superior to
knowledge by description, then one must not only read Kant or
Dreiser, but also hear them speak in their authentic accents. Here
are the ingredients of an argument for preferring cosmopolitan *Galut*
over hothouse Israel.

The flaws in such an argument are fairly obvious. If proponents
of *Torah ve-Hokhmah* regret that our Isaacs turn out overly narrow
and prone to catching Hirschian colds, it is because we have put first
things first and given precedence to their need for insulation. As
Hirsch himself recognizes, the ventilation of Isaac is intermittent
rather than continuous; his cheeks are invigorated by the fresh dry
breezes of Gerar, not by the sulfuric blasts of Sodom. Furthermore the
carriers of alien ideas whom we would influence and by whom we are
liable to be affected are today, both in Israel and America, more likely
to be other Jews than Gentiles. Surely this makes a difference.

Overall, Israeli Orthodox societies are more polarized, hence
more closed in on themselves, than is American Judaism. This may
be the outcome of historical differences: American Jews, be they

---

[24]On Genesis 20:1 (in *The Pentateuch*, trans. Isaac Levy, 2nd ed. [Gates-
head, Isaac Levy 1982] I:341–42). Cf. Rashi to Genesis 20:1.

"right wing" or modern, were rewarded for participation, to a lesser or greater degree, in the civilization of their adopted country; meanwhile Israeli *haredim*, descendants of the inveterate world-shunning *Yishuv ha-Yashan*, were shunted to the periphery of the new Israeli society in the making. Perhaps polarization flows inexorably from the fact that the "neutral" secular Western culture buffers the sharp antagonisms of divergent commitments and beliefs that otherwise render common life intolerable.

Whatever the causes, and despite the occasional insinuation that the aggressively secular Zionist street, backed by the institutions of the state, poses the greater threat to one's religious integrity, it appears to be the consensus of American Orthodoxy that Israel is, with respect to religious education, "safer" than the gilded ghettos of North America. Even those who celebrate the resurgence of Orthodoxy in America, and the success of *yeshivot* in holding the allegiance of their graduates, are wary of overconfidence. Thus, an article that takes issue with religious Zionism asserts, as a matter of course, that "living in a free society is a direct threat to remaining within *Klal Yisrael*."[25] And the confines of Israel better contain the menace of freedom than the disorderly expanses of North America. As for the committed centrist community, I should not be surprised to see our best representatives heading for Israel out of concern for their chil-

---

[25]Yaakov Weinberg: "The Awareness Imperative," *Jewish Observer* 13:7 (Kislev 5739, December 1978): 4–5. Daniel Gutenmacher, "Agudat Israel of America and the State of Israel—The Case of the *Jewish Observer*," in *Israel and Diaspora Jewry*, ed. Eliezer Don-Yehiya, 109–26, collects many relevant texts, most of them from an earlier period than the one I examined. He presents, among others, the view of Rabbi Shelomoh Danziger, according to which the United States is a place "where the *Torah* community is respected and flourishing," while Israel is a place "in which the *Torah* is maligned and psychologically curbed." On *haredi* attitudes to the State of Israel, see A. Ravitzky, "Exile in the Holy Land: The Dilemma of Haredi Jewry," in *Israel: State and Society, 1948–1988*, Studies in Contemporary Jewry, vol. 5, ed. Peter Y. Medding (New York: Oxford University Press, 1989), 89–125.

dren's social development, much as an earlier generation fled the "out of town" rabbinate once the first child approached the watershed of school.

The other side of Israel's sheltered religiosity is the curtailing of those virtues we associate with American-accented Orthodoxy. Generalizing about the Israeli scene, contemplating both the *haredi* and the militantly Zionist brands of Orthodoxy, one recoils from the tendency to intellectual sclerosis, of which the constriction of general education is as much a symptom as a cause; the scotomized morality that cannot but diminish the stature of the piety of which it is the ostensible expression; the sullen resentment that quickens a brooding ideological pugnacity. These deficiencies afflict contemporary Orthodoxy everywhere; indeed they are pandemic to the human condition. Yet the narrow focus, the polemic intensity, and the colorful partisanship of the groups involved raises the spiritual temperature to the point of fever. Hopes that the influx of American *haredim* would temper the Israeli variety and build bridges between the communities, seem to have been exaggerated. *Kima kima batil* seems to be the applicable rule: the indigenous *haredim* set the tone and exert the influence.[26] The looming prospect of cultural claustrophobia is more than merely a restriction of opportunity. Undoubtedly, it leads a significant number of thinking religious individuals to fear for their *klitah tovah* and stay put.

In the final analysis, though, such reservations belong to the realm of individual considerations discussed in the first section of this essay. To the extent that contact with non-Jewish culture and its carriers is, for whatever reason, important for the fulfillment of the Jewish vocation, this can, in principle, be accomplished in Israel. Thus the ventilation factor may play a role in the decision to tarry in *Galut* and add meaning to such an existence. It cannot, however, constitute a self-sustaining theory of *Galut*.

---

[26]See Amnon Levi, "Anglo-Saxon Haredim in Israel: Can They Serve as a Bridge Between Haredim and Secularists?" in *Li-Hiyot be-Yahad*, ed. Charles Liebman (Jerusalem: Keter, 1990), 15–29.

SIN AND PUNISHMENT

Rabbi Bahye's second reason for our dispersion among the nations is that we are punished for our sins: "Israel had sinned in the holy land. . . . Therefore it was decreed that they be exiled. . . . And with the exile and subjugation our iniquities are expurgated. . . ." The theological underpinnings of this conception require no exposition; the textual supports are innumerable, their power augmented by each repetition of *musaf le-yom tov*. Hence the belief that one's life in *Galut* expurgates and expiates our sins would be expected to mold our experience. Why is this, by and large, not the case for American Orthodoxy?

I would distinguish three factors that undermine the position of *mipnei hatta'enu* ("because of our sins") in our community. The first is the general eclipse of the sense of sin in the modern world, with the concomitant decline of belief in the metaphysical reality of punishment. This spiritual and intellectual impoverishment is most evident outside Orthodox Judaism and is even regarded as a mark of spiritual progress. It can hardly be denied, however, that this cultural fashion has swayed many in our community; I believe it has left its mark on the "right wing" world as well. Why this is so and how this tendency should be countered is, however, not directly relevant to our discussion.

The second factor is that religious freedom and material well-being do not quite feel like *Galut*. A rightist spokesman plaintively asks: "Is it enough that we sense *golus* from time to time? Does not the *Shulchan Aruch* demand that the *amah al amah* be located near the doorway, to serve as a constant reminder of our status?"[27] And when *Galut* no longer feels like *Galut*, it certainly, *a fortiori*, does not feel like punishment.

---

[27] Aaron Twerski, "The Stumbling Blocks," *Jewish Observer* 13:7 (Kislev 5739, December 1978), 6–8. For the idea that return to Israel is worthwhile only under ideal conditions, see A. Ravitzky, "Zionism and Messianism in Orthodox Judaism: A Historical and Conceptual Introduction," in *Be-Havlei Masoret u-Temurah*, ed. Menahem Kahane (Rehovot: Kivunim, 1990), 211–44, esp. 212.

Lastly, can we truly think of *Galut* as punishment when we pass up the opportunity to reverse that failure to live rightly in the Land, which is why we were expelled from it in the first place? Beneath the prosperous robes of success may beat the heart of a Daniel, wearing the afflictions of *Galut* like Thomas More's hair shirt, suffering in his or her unique way the agony of individual, national, cosmic alienation and reconciliation with God. Who can penetrate the "reasons of the heart," the mystery of the human individual standing before God? Yet who can deny that, in the ordinary course of events, one who is in pain acts to eradicate the pain, and one who repents seeks to undo the cause of the offense?

In a word, to structure the contemporary experience of privileged *Galut* around the gesture of expiation is rational only in conjunction with a theory, compatible with religious Zionism, explaining why the work of spiritual restoration cannot be better endeavored by renewing our habitation of *Eretz Yisrael*. Such a justification of working for redemption while living in *Galut* could be supplemented by the traditional *mipnei hatta'enu*, though it could presumably stand on its own. Let us consider what such an approach would look like.

GALUT AS REMEDIAL JUDAISM

A possible function of *Galut* is to prepare the Jewish people as a whole, segments of the people, or individuals for the return to Israel. The generation submits to being "the last of subjugation," in the hope that its successor will be "the first of redemption."[28] Note that we do not predicate the argument on its applicability to the entire nation. One segment may be ready, while another is to remain behind, and others could justify their place in *Galut* by reference to the needs of the second. One premise of this position is that the nation is not yet completely ready to resume the destiny envisioned by the Torah; the second is that premature return will hinder rather than help the building up of Land and people.

---

[28]The quoted phrases alter the meaning of a well-known line in Bialik's *Metei Midbar*.

The paradigm for this approach is Rambam's explanation of the children of Israel's initial detour in the desert. Having just emerged from slavery, they were psychologically unprepared for war. Immediate confrontation with the challenge of entering Canaan would be disastrous.[29] Hence, God cunningly avoids guiding the newly liberated slaves "by way of the land of the Philistines." By analogy, one might argue, a sizable number of Jews are not yet ready to make their contribution in Israel, and their going there would be more a bane than a boon, either for themselves or for the nation as a whole.

In Exodus it is God who decides, providentially, to defer the challenge; how does one make such a determination absent the explicit expression of the divine will? Even an anti-Zionist like Rabbi Abraham Mordecai Alter of Gora, while castigating those who celebrate the Balfour Declaration, is unwilling to turn his back on the opportunities it opens up: "But if, by God's Providence, there will be a greater opportunity to settle the Land, then the obligation of settlement is also greater."[30] Of course the same problem arises whenever

---

[29]*Guide* 3:32. Cf. *Meshekh Hokhmah* beginning of *Be-Shallah* on the low immunity to Canaanite religion of the generation that left Egypt. Netziv (*Rinnah shel Torah* 11, to *Shir ha-Shirim* 1:5) states that the Jews were reluctant to return to Israel after the Babylonian Exile because they feared that dwelling in the land would renew the temptation of idolatry. He bases himself on an idiosyncratic interpretation of *Shir ha-Shirim Rabbah* to 5:3, one that contradicts the standard commentators on *Midrash Rabbah*, as well as *Torah Temimah* to 5:3, and diverges from Netziv's own commentary to 5:3. An extreme formulation, according to which the settlement of Israel precipitated an inexorable decline into materialism ("as the land enlarged its cultivation, the intellect enlarged its derogation"), appears in *Hovot ha-Levavot* 9:7, alluding to Deuteronomy 8:12ff.

[30]Cited by Mendel Piekarz, *Hasidut Polin* (Jerusalem: Bialik Institute, 1990), 233. Cf. Hirsch: "So long as God does not call us to the place He had destined for us, to take hold of the land and inheritance as in days immemorial and years of yore, then we are obligated in every place that God chooses for us to dwell in each town and shire in the dwellings of Israel in the exile, to inhabit and live there" (*Horev* 437; see also sections 607–9 and 145).

self-scrutiny becomes a factor in choosing one's destiny. Yet the difficulty is compounded by the material advantages of the fleshpots. Our fellow non-travelers conspire, by force of numbers alone, to make this place assume the permanence of home, while the inertia of a lifetime accumulates atop the inertia of millennia. "Better . . . to stay cowering like this in the early lessons."[31]

Eventually, the heart-stopping moment arrives when it is too late to elude the finality of loss. Not having prepared for the feast, one is, unlike the dying Moses, denied the last benediction and the mountain prospect. "Let what is broken so remain," resolve Tennyson's "Lotos Eaters": "Our sons inherit us, our looks are strange, And we should come like ghosts to trouble joy." A famous thesis of Ibn Ezra belies the optimism implied by Rambam's formulation: "Israel were derelict and unfit for war. . . . And God caused all the males leaving Egypt to die . . . until the generation arose in the desert that had not seen exile."[32]

Adopting the "remedial reading" of our continued, now freely elected, American sojourn, is thus not without psychological cost. Our intuitive distaste toward this way of structuring our existence reflects the sense of personal despair in judging oneself unworthy, consigning oneself to the ranks of those "desert dead," those who do not resemble recumbent giants, who have never dared disturb the gold and silent sands of endless oblivion. There is an additional motive, however, for our repugnance. For the unrestricted application of this principle not only makes us locusts in our own eyes; it also seems to call into question our confidence in the Torah as a source of guidance in the face of forthcoming predicaments.

A bit of history is instructive. The idea that America is a better haven than *Eretz Yisrael*, at least for the time being, goes back to Y. L. Gordon, one of the most outspoken anti-Orthodox leaders of Eastern European *Haskalah*. Going to the Holy Land, in his view, would only

---

[31]John Ashbery, "Soonest Mended," in *The Double Dream of Spring* (New York: Dutton, 1970).

[32]Commentary to Exodus 14:13 (cf. to Exodus 2:3).

perpetuate, nay exacerbate, the collisions between modernity and Rabbinical Judaism that were, in his opinion, the root of many evils. Decades later, when the Mizrachi, under the leadership of Rabbi Reines, supported Herzl's Uganda initiative, they were accused by their cultural adversaries (apparently without an atom of objective evidence), of forsaking Israel because they secretly conceded that the difficulty of constructing a modern Jewish society in accordance with the Torah was too daunting, especially as regards the observance of *shemittah*.[33]

"In exile, Jews are in 'spring training'; the 'regular season' only begins officially when Jews return to their natural homeland."[34] So writes an exponent of religious Zionism, explaining Ramban's doctrine that the Torah is truly fulfilled only in Israel. Perpetuating the exhibition season, for Gordon and his contemporary heirs, is nothing less than an avoidance of championship competition and casts Orthodoxy as the Washington Senators of the Jewish people, anxious to stay cowering like this in the basement of the early lessons, "since the promise of learning is a delusion."

In all honesty, few of us are completely satisfied with the state of halakhic jurisprudence as it affects contemporary society in general and as the "shadow constitution" of the Israeli polity in particular. It is perhaps just as well, at this stage, that *medinat halakhah* (the

---

[33]See Eliezer Don-Yehiya, "Ideology and Policy: R. Reines's Conception of Zionism and the Position of Mizrachi on the Uganda Question," in *Sugyot be-Toledot ha-Tzionut ve-ha-Yishuv 2: Ha-Zerem ha-Dati ba-Tzionut,* ed. Anita Shapira (Tel Aviv: Tel Aviv University Press, 1983), 57–58; and Ehud Luz, *Parallels Meet,* trans. L. J. Schramm (Philadelphia: Jewish Publication Society, 1988), 267–68.

[34]David Hartman, "Zionism and the Continuity of Judaism," in *Joy and Responsibility* (Jerusalem: Ben-Zvi-Posner, 1978), 271. The history of this idea is treated by Aviezer Ravitzky, *Hatzivi Lakh Tziunim—Gilgulo shel Raayon,* in *Eretz Yisrael be-Hagut ha-Yehudit,* ed. M. Hallamish and A. Ravitzky, 1–39; reprinted in Aviezer Ravitzky, *Al Daat ha-Makom* (Jerusalem: Keter, 1991), 34–73.

halakhic state) belongs to the realm of *hilkheta le-meshiha* (utopian *halakhah*); also that, in the absence of "most of her inhabitants," we need not confront the economic revolution attendant upon the reinstitution of halakhic regulations governing real estate transactions and so forth. Perhaps the prolongation of our American settlement is in the best interests of ultimate redemption. No doubt some individuals are destined to make their contribution here. Yet it is far from clear how, by indefinitely deferring our unmediated participation in the Jewish people's rendezvous with destiny, we expect to improve matters.

BY SPIRIT ALONE

The previous approach acknowledges the inferiority of *Galut*. Another perspective favors the *Galut* situation, in spite of its manifest and undeniable evils, over any worldly alternative possible in Israel. The key to this surprising reversal is the contrast of *Galut* as spiritual with the corporeal nature of *avodat ha-Shem* in the Land of Israel.

Long before the rise of Hibbat Zion it was common for hasidic leaders, in the wake of their medieval forerunners, to deploy "*Galut*" as a metaphor for a variety of worldly and spiritual misfortunes. A disciple of the "Holy Jew" states that "whoever serves God has, in his home, an aspect of *Eretz Yisrael*."[35] Rabbi Shneur Zalman of Liady is typical of hasidic writers who wrestled with this notion:

> Therefore the root of the *mitzvot* is precisely in Eretz Israel, and the spies were then at a very high level and they did not wish to lower themselves to the practical *mitzvot* which is the aspect of drawing down the Infinite Light. And they said about Eretz

[35]Cited by Mendel Piekarz, *Hasidut Polin*, 205; see also Rivka Shatz-Uffenheimer, *Ha-Hasidut ke-Mistika* (Jerusalem: Magnes, 1968), 168–77. For medieval roots of this idea in *Kabbalah* and in the Meiri to *Ketubbot* 111a, see I. Twersky, "Maimonides on Eretz Yisrael," 288, n. 46.

Israel that it consumes its inhabitants, for it was their opinion that if the Infinite Light were revealed below as above, their being would be completely abrogated.[36]

Scholars have debated whether the early hasidic appropriation of eschatological themes for spiritual purposes effectively "neutralized" messianic fervor among *hasidim*.[37] The leading authority on later Polish *Hasidut* maintains that the internalizing, pro-*Galut* trend persisted into our century, at least in part, as a negation of Zionist pessimism about Jewish survival and authenticity outside of Israel.[38]

The philosophy of history, according to which the religious destiny of the Jewish people is properly fulfilled only in *Galut*, thus makes its appearance in the work of influential Torah thinkers. The attraction of this position also arises from acquaintance with European civilization. This may come about in two ways: On the one hand, a full awakening to the evils caused by excessive attachment to the nation and its terrestrial aspirations may lead to a principled scorn for the historical arena. "History is a nightmare into which we are trying not to slip," the sensitive Jew might pronounce, inverting the words of Stephen Daedelus.[39] On the other hand, a Jewish thinker like Franz Rosenzweig struggles with the value of history but, precisely for that reason, cannot regard as inessential the exclusion of

---

[36]*Likkutei Torah, Be-midbar Shelah* 36b–37a. Cf. *Sefat Emet, Shelah* 5639 (Tel Aviv, 1980) 92.

[37]Gershom Scholem, "Neutralization of the Messianic Element in Early Hassidism," in *The Messianic Idea in Judaism* (New York: Schocken, 1971), 176–203, criticized by I. Tishby, "The Messianic Idea and Messianic Tendencies in the Growth of Hassidut," *Zion* 32 (1967): 1–45. Emanuel Etkes, in a recent state-of-the-field survey (*Heker ha-Hasidut: Megammot ve-Kivvunim*, in *Madda'ei ha-Yahadut*, 1991, pp. 5–21), regards Scholem's position as the consensus.

[38]Mendel Piekarz, *Hasidut Polin*, 206, and his documentation in chaps. 8–9.

[39]The reference is to Joyce's *Ulysses*, end of the second episode.

the Jewish people from the historical stage. The resolution to this tension between Hegelian philosophy and Jewish eternity is Rosenzweig's doctrine of the double covenant, whereby Christianity pur-
sues the path of history while Judaism, impervious to change and
above history, stands at the goal.[40]

The Zionist rejoinder to the spiritual devaluation of history is
both practical and theological. At one level, involvement in the
vicissitudes of history is unavoidable. We may not be interested in
history, but, whether we like it or not, history (to paraphrase
Trotsky's remark about the dialectic) is *very* interested in us. In this
line of reasoning, brilliantly advanced in Emil Fackenheim's *To Mend
the World*, the Holocaust refutes Rosenzweig, not as one would refute
an assimilationist, by convicting him of unwarranted optimism, but
by demonstrating the sheer unreality of the attempt to exist beyond
historical space. To banish the historical from the existential Jewish
horizon is simply impossible.[41]

Secondly, the neutralization of the political-historical dimension is precisely that—a profound theological re-orientation that
commandeers a substantial corpus of Torah, presumed to address the
earthly destiny of the Jew, and projects it into the possession of an
inner, spiritualized domain. With all due regard for the value and
power of this allegorization, it cannot replace the original meaning.
Halakhah is hopelessly wed to terrestrial obligations and ideals. The
original blueprint envisioned by the Torah, according to which Israel
was to occupy its homeland and never undergo exile, was not a tem-

---

[40]See Ehud Luz, "Zionism and Messianism in the Thought of Franz
Rosenzweig," *Mehkerei Yerushalayim be-Mahshevet Yisrael* 2:3 (1983): 472–
89, and literature cited there; also S. Moses, "Franz Rosenzweig vis-à-vis
Zionism," in *Ha-Tzionut u-Mitnaggedeha ba-Am ha-Yehudi*, ed. Haim Avni
(Jerusalem: Zionist Library, 1990), 321–28.

[41]For Orthodox critique of Rosenzweig, see Eliezer Berkovits, *Major
Themes in Modern Philosophies of Judaism* (New York: Ktav, 1974) and my
review essay on Berkovits, "Modern Jewish Philosophy: Fossil or Ferment?"
Tradition 15:3 (Fall 1975): 142–45.

porary detour from her religious vocation; on the contrary, it is *Galut* that marks a deviation from the Divine plan.

For these reasons it is difficult to quarrel with Professor Blidstein's diagnosis:

> I, for one, am not willing to take at face value the claim that the situation described is simply another instance of the classic tension between Torah (or spirituality) and nationalism. It is much more likely that we are witness to a (no less classic) skewering of Jewish spirituality itself, a communal accommodation to stability and ease.[42]

To grasp this point from a different angle we need look no further than the passage from *Likkutei Torah* with which we introduced this section. Rabbi Shneur Zalman exhibits remarkable sympathy for the spies who were on a very high level and feared that entering Israel would abrogate their being. It is his greatness, and that of much hasidic homiletics at their best, to give voice to the powerful temptation the spies' spirituality represents, despite the clear rejection of their actions and attitudes by the Torah. For he knows very well that the position of the spies is rejected. This sense of complexity suggests a final, more satisfactory way of valorizing the *Galut* experience.

A VALE OF SOUL-MAKING

On the one hand, *Galut* is the negation of normal Jewish life. On the other hand, *Galut* is ordained by God, if not antecedently then consequently.[43] From the eschatological perspective nothing is accidental; the regressions and digressions of history, utterly transformed,

---

[42]*Tradition* 18:1 (Summer 1979): 12.

[43]A kindred view animates Maharal of Prague's theology of *Galut*, e.g., *Netzah Yisrael*, chap. 30. Exile is bad for the Jews but necessary for the dialectic of history.

are seen to be integral parts of the redemptive pattern. Thus *Galut* is a tragic but essential moment in the providential plan. The true, comprehensive account of *Galut* eschews easy evaluations. Recognizing in *Galut* a radical, ultimately intolerable dislocation of the Jewish people, we allow that *Galut* has, nonetheless, enriched our spirits as surely as it has vitiated our lives.

Rabbi Kook exemplifies the search for such theological equilibrium, as illustrated by the following passage:

> In the nation's great trouble itself, when the bustle of national life and its injurious commotion were removed from her midst, the spiritual light began to rise slowly in its midst up the steps it had descended. The spirit of the nation took wing to the degree that it retired from political life, which is the first thing to become impure in a corrupt community.[44]

Galut is neither to be deemed an ideal escape from the terrestrial aspect of human life, nor given up as an existential limbo in which Jews are to "graze until they become unfit" and can be released from their aimless succession of motions. Truly it is abnormal. But a temporal island of abnormality, a nation that has learned that its vocation depends neither on force of arms nor cohesion of territory, is better for the purgative experience. This approach potentially incorporates, of course, the themes articulated by the other approaches we have listed. It thus brings to the end of this part of our discussion the virtue of comprehensiveness.

III

To this point we have worked within the limits of the questions: Why do we find ourselves in *Galut*? What might our job in *Galut* possibly be? We have used this inquiry to shed light on our subject, namely,

---

[44]"Land and Spirit," from the introduction to *Shabbat ha-Aretz*, reprinted in *Hazon ha-Geullah* (Jerusalem, 1941), 53. Similar formulations abound in Rabbi Kook's earlier (e.g., "The Way of Renaissance" in *Maamrei*

how we experience our lives in *Galut*. From these possibilities, it is time to pass to the present situation of the American Jew who is a card-carrying member of the religious Zionist "foreign legion." Can we identify characteristics of our experience that cut across our individual peculiarities, beyond the bare bones of the categories examined above? Needless to say, any answer to this question inevitably entails prescriptive judgments as well.

As indicated at the outset, many differences between life in America and in Israel are not suitable candidates, however important they might be for individuals and groups, for our discussion. Two of them are important enough to deserve explicit dismissal. One is the general level of material status. Moving to Israel, for most Americans, given their advantageous financial and educational backgrounds, is not inviting the wolf to the door. The quality of material life for the vast majority of Israelis, too, is incomparably higher than it was three or four decades ago: automobiles, leisure appurtenances, foreign travel are taken for granted today, as telephones, central heating, refrigerators, and even indoor toilets, were not, then. To be sure, as noted, what one person is indifferent to, another desires and a third cannot live without; we are also, I presume, right in thinking that typical Israelis must hustle more than we to get the money to buy their things. It seems to me, however, that the contrast in quality of material life and possessions is not as stark as we are accustomed to imagine it—in any event one of degree rather than one of kind.

---

ha-Reiyah [Jerusalem, 5740]) and later (e.g., "War" in *Orot* [Jerusalem: Mossad Harav Kook, 1961]) writings. See also *Orot*, 102–18. Cf. n. 29. Rabbi Chaim Steinmetz has directed me to the earlier views of Rabbi Yosef Yaavetz and Rabbi Raphael Berdugo, according to whom Exile enabled the Jewish people to avoid the temptations of material preoccupation and to cultivate the life of the spirit. See Dan Manor, *Galut u-Geullah be-Hagut Hakhmei Morocco ba-Meot ha17–18* (Lod: Haberman Institute, 1988), 106. But note as well Berdugo's more conventionally negative views of exile (Ibid., 48).

The second issue, that of security, is far more complex, for reasons that are significant for the further development of our inquiry. At first blush the debate cuts both ways. People who walk the streets of New York are easily made reluctant to visit Israel (or permit their children to study there) on account of the political situation. Meanwhile, Mayor Lahat of Tel Aviv carries with him the memory of being mugged on Broadway. For Americans, Israel sounds like Dodge City; for Israelis, American Jews (for that matter other Americans too) are defenseless victims.

If this were the entire story, the estimation of comparative security could be consigned, for all practical purposes, to the calculations of insurance salesmen. Yet there is a sense in which the threat to Israeli Jews cuts deeper, and plays a more comprehensive role in our self-definition, than the parallel fears that take up residence in the minds of Western Jews. It may be worth our while to explore the asymmetry at two distinct levels:

1. The American Jew, nervously scanning the crime statistics, rightly or wrongly fears violation of his or her person, family, fellow Jews, or fellow men, as individuals. Even if Jewishness heightens the likelihood of being attacked, even when anti-Semitism appears as a motive for crime, the menace is essentially private. When a series of incidents leads Jews to speak of a "neighborhood under siege," we are using a metaphor, and we know it. Israeli Jews, by contrast, are imperiled collectively. This is both a reflection of the unique status of *Eretz Yisrael* for Judaism and for Jews, and an obvious consequence of the empirical situation. In any event, the Israeli experience is, I believe, different in quality from the former.[45]

---

[45]A loose halakhic analogy may illustrate the qualitative distinction between collective danger and risk to individuals. See *Shabbat* 42a (and the ruling at *Orah Hayyim* 334:27) on extinguishing a live coal, or capturing a venomous snake, on the Sabbath. Rashba, treating the possibility that the distinction applies even *d'Oraita*, argues that danger to the community is to be met head on ("since its nature is to cause damage and the populace

2. More important is the difference in the experience of responsibility. In the final analysis, the Israeli must regard that which
befalls the community as a challenge to the community's action and
initiative. Disputes about relative security, therefore, are more than a
matter of actuarial tables or psychological projection. They are
rather about the central attitudes underlying the existential character of Israeli life as distinguished from our experience of *Galut*.[46]

We must therefore focus on the deeper outlook that manifests
itself in differing conceptions of responsibility for the Jewish people.
Religious Zionists believe that living in Israel is not simply an opportunity to fulfill more *mitzvot* (though, as noted before, that is an incentive for all religious Jews). They are united, at a deeper level, by
the conviction that Israel is where great things are in the making,
that they are called upon to take part in the shaping of that history,
and that the common life of Jews living in Israel has enormous significance for the destiny of *klal Yisrael*.

Jews living in America, by contrast, may be profoundly committed to their own spiritual welfare, to the welfare (spiritual and material) of their community, even to that of non-Orthodox and assimi-
lated Jews. Their sense of communal responsibility may extend to
active concern for the welfare of American society. The enterprise
partakes, however, at a certain level, of classic American "voluntary-
ism." As individuals, or as a community, we do not ordinarily con-

---

is harmed, Samuel considers it like danger to life, for the many cannot be
sufficiently careful, for if one is careful, yet the other will not guard himself"), whereas in the case of risk to individuals the persons concerned are
to remove themselves from harm's way rather than removing the source of
the harm. (See also *Maggid Mishneh* to *Hilkhot Shabbat* 10:17.)

[46]My revision of this section is indebted to Rabbi Lichtenstein's comments. It was also enriched by the Gulf War crisis, during which Israel, for
the first time, was exposed to attack without being able to respond actively, thus underscoring the conceptual distinction between the two
levels of asymmetry in the text.

ceive of our actions reverberating down the corridors of recorded time. We may wish to conceive of ourselves responding to the cosmic, eschatological challenge, but when we try, we often end up feeling more comical than heroic. The morally relevant distinction of the gilded *Galut* fleshpots, like those of Egypt, is the word *hinnam*, that is, free of *mitzvot*. This freedom, for Orthodox Jews, does not take the form of respite from the observance of the Torah. Instead it is reflected in a more relaxed attitude toward the challenge of national responsibility.

The second aspect of the security question, to which we alluded before, is best thought of in this context. The Herzlian hope that Israel would solve, once and for all, the "troubles of the Jews," seems more illusory than ever in a country surrounded by, and infested by, mortal enemies. The physical threat has not been eliminated. It has, however, been transformed. The Israeli realizes that the common-wealth, meaning himself, is responsible for his security as a Jew. He is expected, nay required, to do his share in the army; government policy is presumed to reflect his direct participation as a Jew. It is thus difficult for him to pretend that what happens in his country has nothing to do with his actions. Quite patriotic American Orthodox Jews—as well as other Jews, as well as other Americans of our general socioeconomic status—can live in a democracy that enters a military engagement, and express their opinion of government policy, without personally knowing anyone who will fight in that war. We read about racially motivated boycotts of Korean stores without feeling that we *must*, as citizens and as commemorators of our grandparents' blood, do more than shake our heads and avert our eyes.

It is remarkable that we do not feel more uncomfortable about this degree of detachment than we do. This may be due, as Charles Liebman has argued, to the profoundly apolitical, therapeutic nature of the American upper middle classes.[47] We may also feel relatively at

---

[47]"Changing Conceptions of Political Life and their Implications for American Judaism," in *Public Life in Israel and the Diaspora*, ed. Sam Lehman-Wilzig and Bernard Susser (Ramat Gan: Bar-Ilan University Press, 1981), 91–100.

home amid the widespread transience of American culture, hence unafraid that we will be singled out as an alien presence, squatters in someone else's fatherland.[48]

The roots of this difference between Israel and Exile are both theological and historical. The metaphysical divergence in self-conception goes back to *Tanakh*. While both individual and communal responsibility play a role throughout biblical theodicy, it is no accident that it is Ezekiel—educating the people for religious life in *Galut* —who preaches the emphasis on individual responsibility more explicitly than any other prophet.[49] Nor is it an accident that the fullness of communal responsibility comes into force only with the entry into Israel and, according to one view, is suspended with the destruction of the Second Temple.[50] A sense of communal destiny seems metaphysically appropriate to Israel, while spiritual individualism would reflect the realities of life in the Diaspora.

The historical factors can be divided into issues of ideology and matters of circumstance. If religious Zionism aspires to redemptive action to transform the state of the Jewish people materially and to attain those spiritual achievements possible only through renewed communal life in the Land, then it is only understandable that those who are most committed will be the ones to make *aliyah*. At the same time the situation in which these individuals find themselves con-

---

[48]Could a leading American politician say of Henry Kissinger, for example, what Xavier Vallat said about the tragedy for France, that it should be led by a man (Premier Leon Blum) whose "race was condemned by divine malediction never to have a motherland"? (David Clay Large, *Between Two Fires: Europe's Path in the 1930's* [New York: Norton, 1990], 329). It is not so much the venom that is lacking as the very vocabulary.

[49]See chaps. 14, 18, and 33 and cf. Jeremiah 31. The rabbis (*Makkot* 24a) already identified Ezekiel as the distinct spokesman for individual responsibility. I have dealt with this issue in detail in my lectures on Ezekiel.

[50]*Sanhedrin* 43b and Rabbi Levi in *Sotah* 7:5; I am interpreting Rabbi Levi against the *Korban ha-Edah*, in agreement with Rabbi S. Goren, *Torat ha-Moadim* (Tel Aviv: Avraham Zion, 5724), 69f.

tinually provides them with occasions for renewed commitment. The *Yishuv* has indeed had to cope with large waves of *klitah*, with constant military requirements, with the demand to formulate and act decisively on its understanding of the new state's identity and future, with the tensions of coexistence between religious and nonreligious. Those who are not crushed by the burden can only be fortified in their resolution.

The distinctive circumstances of Israeli Jewry are not limited to the extraordinary requirements of crisis situations. The conditions of ordinary life are also dissimilar in ways that make for a greater sense of responsibility. For one thing, all Jews are identifiable as Jews and receive an education that, however impoverished by our standards, creates something of a common language. No American institution provides a sense of collective fate comparable to that inculcated by service in *Tzahal*. The average American Jew is virtually incapable of imagining what it is like to refrain from work on *Shabbat*. His or her Israeli counterpart in Tel Aviv has seen *Shabbat* observed as a public day of rest.[51] There is no way to drop out of the Jewish people, short of emigration. All of these factors reinforce the sense that other Jews' spiritual destiny is very much a part of one's own.

This brief characterization of the Israeli spiritual horizon is open to question from both theological and historical perspectives. We shall not rehearse the many issues of conflict between religious Zionists and the non-Zionist Orthodox. Accepting the view that Jews are not obligated, are even enjoined from, returning to the Land must necessarily affect how we experience our being in *Galut*. It is not clear how widely and strongly such a position is held. At any rate, it is less

---

[51]Cf. "As for Tel Aviv, the 'town of speculators,' which most Zionists view as a questionable Zionist achievement—I cannot help being impressed by the fact that all stores there close from *Kiddush* to *Havdalah*, and that thus, at any rate, the mold into which the content of the Sabbath can flow is provided. Where could we find that here!," *Franz Rosenzweig: His Life and Thought*, ed. Nahum Glatzer (New York: Schocken, 1961), 357 (letter to Benno Jacob).

pervasive, and less debilitating, than the attempt to live in Israel while resisting this sense of responsibility. Such a position is maintained when one declines to recognize the majority of Israeli Jews as significant limbs in the body of *knesset Yisrael*, or regards the Jews of Israel as either numerically or spiritually insignificant compared to the Jewish people outside of Israel.

Elements of such a view are expressed, to some degree, in the non-Zionist Orthodox world. One need not burn the Israeli flag to adopt such an approach. It is quite compatible with wishing Israel well, even beyond the minimal awareness that "in its peace is your peace." All it takes is the kind of detachment, critical or benign, that constitutes the prevalent spectator attitude toward social and political life in America. Because it is easy to slip into attitudes typical of *Galut*, and because we share many of the criticisms that fuel the gesture of detachment on the part of the *haredi* world, this is a temptation that religious Zionists must assiduously resist.

As noted above, the sense of responsibility characteristic of religious Zionism as lived in Israel is reinforced by certain features of the contemporary culture. Were those circumstances to alter for the worse, the experience of responsibility would inevitably be affected. Such would be the case, in terms of relations between religious and secular Jews, were the educational gap to increase, or, as seems not impossible,[52] were the public profile of religious observance to shrink substantially. Abatement of the state of perpetual crisis might also diminish the sense of communal responsibility solidified by consciousness of real and urgent demands.

In addition, a weakening of *gemeinschaft* may be the result of certain seemingly value-neutral processes. In a relatively small society it is hard to remain oblivious to your fellow man's concerns. In a mass society it is literally impossible to care deeply about all of one's neighbors. Commitment is inevitably rationed, and the most reasonable form of rationing is to pay attention to your own immediate proxim-

---

[52]See Naomi Cohen, "Israel as a Jewish State," in *Religious Zionism*, ed. Shubert Spero and Yitzchak Pessin, 234–53.

ity and to people who are most like yourself. Thus the attraction of
the Zionist ideal may depend on the society's success in maintaining
the external circumstances that enhance moral capacity.[53]

IV

If my analysis is correct, cultivating the right kind of concern for *klal
Yisrael* is both the key to motivating religious *aliyah* and to making
that *aliyah* a boon to the community. The preceding discussion may
help us sort out some of the outstanding problems facing us in
Galut—both in our daily lives and inasmuch as we seek to create an
environment helpful to *aliyah*.

1. Should religious Zionism adopt the hard line and view attitudes toward *aliyah* as the criterion dividing authentic from inauthen-
tic Jews? If my analysis is correct, living in Israel is an important
dimension of one's spiritual identity but does not take the place of
the "perennial" Jewish virtues cultivated throughout *Galut*. The living ideals of contemporary Orthodoxy, in Israel and in *Galut*, are
those that have animated God-fearing Jews for millennia: commitment to Torah and concern for the Jewish people. An individual educated to this double ideal will naturally appreciate the value of dwelling in Israel, the *mitzvot* that can be fulfilled only upon its soil, the
unique challenges of its edification in this our time. His commitment
to Israel need not derive from indoctrination in the belief that spiritual excellence is inconceivable outside of Israel, that only the *oleh*
eludes a shadowy, vicarious religious existence. To the contrary, his
commitment is built on the same foundations that will sustain his
spirit if he chooses, for whatever considerations, to make his life in
Galut.

At first blush, this approach appears to be unexceptional. Yet
there has been a tendency among some modern Orthodox educators
to put all their religious eggs in the Israel basket, assuming that only
nationalism has a chance to secure the loyalties of their pupils for

---

[53]See, above, the epigraph from Rabbi Kook.

authentic Judaism. Furthermore, vigorous uncompromising religious Zionism can overcome feelings of religious inferiority vis-à-vis Agudah circles, by locating an area of religious observance in which we Mizrachists can put them to shame.[54]

The consequences of this putative religious "specialization" on the part of religious Zionists have been unfortunate. Those who subscribe to it are tempted to inappropriate disparagement of Orthodox segments on the right, both dismissing piety that is not committed to *aliyah* and signifying that only Zionist motives for dwelling in Israel bear spiritual value, thus implying, it would seem, that Hazon Ish and the Brisker Rav lacked *ahavat ha-aretz*! By the same token, militant

---

[54]The desire to measure up to the Agudah world in some area was presumably a factor in Mafdal's journey to the territorial right wing. See Shmuel Sandler, "The National Religious Party: Towards a New Role in Israel's Political System?," in *Public Life in Israel and the Diaspora*, ed. Sam Lehman-Wilzig and Bernard Susser (Ramat Gan: Bar-Ilan University Press, 1981), 164. On the question of effective education to Zionist realization, I am pleased to note the convergence of my outlook with the observations of Rabbi Jonathan Sacks, "Religious and National Identity—British Jewry and the State of Israel," in *Israel and Diaspora Jewry*, ed. Eliezer Don-Yehiya, 53–60. The chief rabbi mentions the high *aliyah* rate from British communities that are not "Israel-oriented to any significant degree," contrasting it with what he perceives as the bewilderment felt by South African educators "who constructed the most outstanding Israel-centered secondary-school movement, and are currently witnessing the mass emigration of the products of those schools, not to Israel but to Australia and Canada." He goes on to characterize the most significant impetus to *aliyah* as "a way of life in which one is prepared to make sacrifices for the sake of one's Jewishness, in which one lives in a state of tension between one's Jewishness and the environment, and in which that tension has a significantly negative value," 58–59.

[55]For a hilariously sad example of a failed attempt to bridge unilaterally, through hard-line nationalistic rhetoric, the gap between a Borsht Belt comedian and battle-weary Israeli soldiers, see Jackie Mason with Ken Gross, "Too Jewish," in *Jackie Oy!* (Boston: Little, Brown, 1988), 187–98.

political positions become the equivalent of the conspicuous *humrah*. This is worse in the United States than in Israel, for Americans need not temper their maximalism with reality; to the contrary, the fact that their fervor is that of the spectator virtually compels them to prove through rhetoric and money what is not achieved by direct personal action.[55] Whence the truth of Rabbi Amital's observation that Kahane could claim more support in Queens than in Israel.[56] Among the consequences, of course, is the despair, the resigned acquiescence to a life of spiritual mediocrity, that lies in wait for those who, whether despite their ideological focus or because they balk at the hard sell, fail to make *aliyah*, but who have neglected to build up their other spiritual resources.

Another phenomenon, distinct but not disjunct from the preceding factor, is a tendency to lay down a strict definition of religious Zionism. The fine points of *at'halta de-geulla*, the details of how to observe Yom ha-Atzma'ut, the .hypothetical circumstances under which one might be prepared to consider territorial compromise in *Yesha* (Judea, Samaria, and Gaza) are sometimes treated as litmus tests of acceptability. Doing so engenders unnecessary divisiveness within Orthodoxy, on the one hand, while obscuring what ought to be the real distinction between us and the *haredi* world, on the other hand—namely the question of responsibility based on a sense of relationship to the Jewish people as broadly defined.

2. Responsibility toward the Jewish people normally goes hand in hand with the ability to identify with its members. Not separating oneself from the *tzibbur* is more than a matter of actions but includes emotional participation in the community's adversity as well.[57] Yet sometimes the true mark of solidarity is the ability to share in the community's life when trouble is no longer nigh. As Nietzsche shrewdly observes: "Fellowship in joy, and not sympathy in sorrow,

---

[56]Interestingly, Conor Cruise O'Brien, in "A Tale of Two Nations," *New York Review of Books* 37:12 (July 19, 1990): 35, also chose Queens as the locale where the IRA is more popular than in Ireland.

[57]Rambam, *Hilkhot Teshuvah* 3:11.

makes people friends."[58] For this reason it would appear desirable that those who prepare to live in Israel, and otherwise be concerned with its inhabitants, school themselves in the culture of Israel, in all its variety, high and low, religious and secular.

Needless to say it is nonsense to dash frantically about, trying to master various cultural activities and avocations simply because they are of interest to other people. Any particular elective feature of culture can be dispensed with without damaging the fabric of the Jewish people. Must we commiserate with the Israeli public when a basketball star sprains his ankle or goes AWOL from the team? Are falafel and folk-dancing, once the prophylactic of choice against juvenile assimilation, essential ingredients of vicarious Israelihood?

A moment's reflection on ordinary human relations, however, reveals the hollowness of this objection. Friendship and love are rooted in sympathy regarding essential matters; yet the glue that solidifies adherence, on a day-to-day basis, is often a tie with little inherent significance: the memory of a tune, a joke, a hobby. The symbolic power of such a tie cannot always be predicted, let alone prescribed, but without it commitments often become too fragile to serve their purpose. The same is true of the life of a community and a nation: a measure of overlapping cultural literacy can often, in times of crisis as in times of calm, provide the context in which great ideals are pursued.

How Israelis grapple with the great ideals in which their lives are enmeshed is a worthy subject for penetrating study. My impression is that we Americans lavish disproportionate attention on Israeli politicians as bearers of the national *geist*. We might consider looking at other cultural expressions as well: literature, for example. Much writing emanating from Orthodox circles resonates to the thrust and

---

[58]Friedrich Wilhelm Nietzsche, *Human, All Too Human*, ed. O. Levy, trans. H. Zimmern (New York: Macmillan, 1924), 358. Cf. Samuel Johnson, *Rambler* 64. Of course, Johnson's conception of friendship assumes intensely shared personal interests: hence, greater sensitivity than is tolerable in any broad community.

parry of the polemical marketplace; as a result, it tends to be
hortatory or invective. Literature restores the subtle, living complexity that is often lost in the effort to be politically correct and to get
in the last word. Thus, to take our own topic as an example, we are
inclined to simplify motivations for *aliyah*, to paper over ambivalence,
and to view everything from the perspective of the spiritual ideal.
Nathan Shaham's *Rosendorf Quartet*, to take a recent novel, exhibits
the very mixed feelings of German *olim* in the 1930s, whose spiritual
allegiance belongs to the German artistic tradition, for whom Pales-
tine is little more than a musically underdeveloped outpost at the
edge of Europe, a (temporary?) haven in a time of trouble. Among
those writing from an Orthodox vantage point, Agnon's haunting
story *Ad Olam*, according to one plausible interpretation, reflects a
profound nostalgia for the intellectually pure world of isolation and
exile, the world in which sunset is always more beautiful than sunrise.
We lose touch with these elements of our consciousness, and that of
other Jews, to our own loss and theirs.

3. American Orthodoxy's inability to resolve fully the ambiguity of our relation to Gentiles has consequences for our experience of
Galut and of potential redemption. Clearly, as the *rav* often put it, we
are both strangers and residents (*ger ve-toshav*) in the United States.
It is important that we do not feel at home in *Galut*. It is also difficult
to maintain that feeling when "America's openness and the sociological changes of the past few decades have permitted even the fully
observant Jew to enter the mainstream of American society, and still
faithfully observe *mitzva kala k'chamura*."[59]

One way of keeping alive a sense of *Galut* in America is to incul-
cate an instinctive snideness toward "their" culture, from baseball to
apple pie. Another is to limit, as a matter of principle, active concern
for the affairs of American society, to cultivate a studied *schadenfroh*
toward the moral adversities that rock it. This is, of course, easier for
those segments of Orthodoxy that categorically reject Western cul-

---

[59]S. Glick, "Missing—A Feeling of *Galut*," *Jewish Observer* 14:3 (*Tishre*
5740, October 1979): 13–14.

ture, though here too, there may be much self-deception. For those of
us more open to what the culture has to offer and more willing, in
principle, to seek its welfare, the equilibrium between the estrangement of the sojourner and the civic face of the citizen remains elusive.

The most forceful way of nursing an awareness of *Galut*, however, is to dwell on anti-Semitism. For Dr. Glick, referring to a new
crop of *yeshivah* graduates *not* oriented to Zionism, "complacency
about life in *Galut* is shattered only by Black-Jewish confrontation."[60]
In the waning years of the twentieth century, as other sources of
authority have lost their power, victimhood has come into its own.[61]
Members of groups with access to some significant grievance find it
convenient to be judged not by the color of their skin, nor by the content of their character, but by the size of the chip on their shoulder.
Precisely for this reason, Zionist propagandists are not averse to ham-
mering away at the *Halakhah le-Mosheh mi-Sinai* that "Esau hates
Jacob." I need not remind you that our mistrust of the Gentile world
is amply justified by history and present reality.

One cannot help sensing that a preoccupation with being hated
benefits neither our self-knowledge nor our security. For the love and
fear of God, it substitutes, as the foundation of Jewish identity, a culture of resentment. An obsession with "us versus them" fuels extremism within the Jewish community. How this occurs has been brilliantly described by Shelby Steele, writing of contemporary black
intellectuals:

> To carry off inversion we must become self-conscious about the
> meaning of our race, we must redefine that meaning, invest it
> with an ideology and a politics, claim an essence for it, and
> look to it, as much as to ourselves, as a means of betterment.
> And, of course, this degree of racial preoccupation prepares
> the ground for intense factionalism within the race. Who has

---

[60]Ibid.
[61]See Richard Sennett, *Authority* (New York: Knopf, 1980).

the best twist on blackness, the Black Muslims or the civil rights establishment, the cultural nationalists or the black Baptists, Malcolm X or Martin Luther King? And who is the most black, who the least? Within each faction is a racial orthodoxy that must be endlessly debated and defended, which rallies the faction against other factions while imposing a censorship of thought on its own members.[62]

Let us not dismiss the Jewish version of this ethnic inversion as a deformation of our characters due to *Galut* and readily remedied through *aliyah*. "Israel against the world" is a powerful enough rallying cry to discourage a more nuanced analysis.[63]

One last problem facing the religious Zionist community in America is that of the brain drain. Many of America's best Orthodox intellectual and social resources, in all age groups, now reside in Israel. Israel's gain has been our loss. The inevitable effect has contributed to the weakening of centrist Orthodoxy in this country. In addition to the difficulties this raises for our continued identity as an Orthodox community with an outlook different from that of other Orthodox groups, it also calls into question our ability, in America,

---

[62]*The Content of Our Characters* (New York: St. Martin's Press, 1990), 160. Steele objects to this preoccupation because he believes that it no longer corresponds to the situation of middle-class blacks in the United States: "[T]he American black, supported by a massive body of law and the not inconsiderable goodwill of his fellow citizens, is basically as free as he or she wants to be. For every white I have met who is a racist, I have met twenty more who have seen me as an equal. And of those twenty, ten have only wished me the best as an individual." Hence he opposes the "religion" of black separatism. Here our position vis-à-vis Judaism differs: for us, separation is literally part of our religion, not something to be dropped for the sake of admission to the middle class.

[63]So, too, the tendency of militant American *Olim* to think of Arabs as if they were American blacks, with the difference that now *we* have the guns.

to confront those challenges of contemporary life to which we are best suited, for whatever reasons, to formulate a response. One illustration suffices: despite the influx of many exemplary individuals of the first and second rank, Israel has not produced an educational institution combining the scope and depth of Yeshiva University. Israel is unlikely to do so in the near future. It is not in the interest of religious Judaism that the vigor of Yeshiva be sapped; yet it is unfair to expect individuals who desire to make their lives in Israel to linger any longer than they deem necessary in the country of their exile. I offer no solution to this dilemma.

V

To the Torah Jew who is also heir to the traditions of Western culture, a knock on the door awakens, willy nilly, two lines of association. The first proceeds from the exegesis of Song of Songs 5: "The voice of my Beloved knocks." The speaker has retired for the night; having washed her feet, she delays long enough so that, when she finally turns the doorknob, the Beloved has withdrawn. This haunting image recurs in later Jewish thought. For Rabbi Yehudah Halevi, it tells the story of sixth-century B.C.E. Babylonian Jewry, a community that could have returned to Israel but did not do so.[64] In our own day, this passage is the foundation of *maran ha-Rav's* analysis of American Orthodoxy's responsibility in the first decade of Israel's existence.[65] In between, the reluctance of the speaker to soil her cleansed feet has symbolized the purified spirit, loath to reinvest itself in worldly strivings.[66] The second association takes us back to Lady Macbeth. Appalled by the sound of knocking as they wash up after the murder of Duncan, she bids her husband: "Get on your nightgown, lest occasion call us, and show us to be watchers."

---

[64]*Kuzari* II, 24.

[65]*Kol Dodi Dofek*, in *Be-Sod ha-Yahid ve-ha-Yahad* (Jerusalem: Orot, 5736), 354ff.

[66]E.g., *Toledot Yaakov Yosef* to *Vayera*.

The Macbeths must avoid being exposed as watchers when they would feign sleep. The Jew in exile must avoid, at all costs, being *merely* a spectator. Lest occasion call us, and show us to be watchers, we must move from the periphery of history to its center. Our awareness of the goal may outstrip our capacity to act and thus engender great pain and anxiety. How the individual or the community are to make of opportunity the work of redemption, within the limits of the concrete situation, is ultimately as enigmatic as the human will. It is the proper subject of study and prayer. Thus attempting to define the differences between religious life in Israel and America and the problems facing us in the West cannot exempt us from the unavoidable meeting with the most familiar, yet most elusive, mystery, namely ourselves.[67]

---

[67]My thanks to Chaim I. Waxman, who, as chairman of the Third Orthodox Forum, solicited the paper. I am most grateful for the remarks of my teacher, Rabbi Aharon Lichtenstein, on the first draft, which precipitated the revision of one section. Other helpful comments came from Judith Bleich, Dov Fogel, Moshe Simon, and Rabbi Chaim Steinmetz, who showed me his notes for a lecture on "Exile and Redemption" delivered under the auspices of the Gruss Kollel of Yeshiva University, Spring 1991.

2

Does Place Make a Difference?: Jewish Orthodoxy in Israel and the Diaspora

Eliezer Don-Yehiya

Perceptions of religious values and forms of religious behavior are substantially influenced by the social and political conditions in which they find themselves. This is evident in the marked variations that prevail within the same religious group that is exposed to disparate environmental influences. This essay explores the influence of circumstantial factors on religious perceptions by comparing Orthodox Judaism in Israel with Orthodoxy as conceived and practiced in the Diaspora.

It is worth noting at the outset that the very focus of this essay highlights a basic difference between Israel and the Diaspora. The very term "Orthodox Judaism," which is so accepted among Diaspora Jews, is not commonly used in Israel. Its place is taken by the far more prevalent term "religious Judaism" (*Yahadut datit*). The difference between these two terms is more than merely semantic. It is symptomatic of important differences in the social conditions and political culture that obtain in the two realities. The term "religious Judaism" is rooted in a reality in which those Jews who would be described as Orthodox in the United States and other Western states, perceive themselves and are perceived by other Israelis as the only authentic representatives of religious Judaism. This contrasts with the Western states in which Orthodoxy is considered to be only one of the constituent parts of Judaism. To be sure, even in the United States many Orthodox are unwilling to recognize the Reform and Conservative movements as legitimate representatives of Judaism. Nevertheless, in practice, they must resign themselves to a reality in which Orthodoxy is perceived as only one of the expressions of a "pluralist Judaism."

This difference is expressed in the political preeminence that is granted to the Orthodox conception of Jewish religious tradition in Israel and is one of the reasons for Orthodoxy's practical control over several areas of Israeli public life. This preeminence is, to a large extent, a consequence of the prevailing view that understands Orthodoxy as the most authentic representation of Judaism. Notably, many of those who hold to this view do not lead Orthodox lives. Significantly, they define themselves as "secular" or "traditional"—these terms alluding to a low level of affect for the Jewish religion rather than to a different interpretation of Jewish tradition.

This tendency is most especially manifest in the attitudes of the so-called "traditional" (*Mesorati*) circles in Israel. Undeniably, there is much in common between the behavior patterns of these "traditional" Israeli Jews and of non-Orthodox groups in Western states— such as the American Conservative movement. And yet, even though the Conservative movement in Israel describes itself as the "Movement for Traditional Judaism," it is quite distinct from that very large group of Israelis who define themselves as "traditional." Interestingly, this difference does not consist of their respective degree of rigorous religious observance. Rather, it involves the willingness evinced by these two groups to ascribe religious legitimacy to behavior patterns that depart from the halakhic norm. The Israeli traditionals, as opposed to the principled Conservatives and Reform, do not find it appropriate to ascribe religious legitimacy to their deviations from Orthodox practices. Neither do they give organizational expression to their behavior patterns by establishing special synagogues geared to their religious practices and headed by rabbis of "their kind." These groups are unwilling to challenge the authority of the Orthodox rabbinate in regard to the proper interpretation of religious law. Although their behavior departs from the halakhic norm and approximates to that of the Conservative or the Reform, their religious point of reference remains Orthodox in character.

The especial prominence of "traditionalism" in Israel is one of the central differences between Orthodoxy in Israel and in the Western states. The cause for the marginal influence of non-Orthodox movements is, therefore, not to be found only or mainly in the peculiarities that mark Israel's legal framework or in the character of its political arrangements. The relevant fact is that those who are close to these non-Orthodox movements in their religious behavior patterns are for the very most part unwilling to organize in the support of a religious alternative. It is significant that in contrast to contemporary Diaspora Jews, non-Orthodox Israelis do not need alternative forms of religious affiliation in order to affirm their Jewish identity, which is largely expressed in national-political terms. This is one of the main reasons that only a negligible minority among the Israeli Jews belong to Conservative or Reform congregations, and these are, in very large part, immigrants who came to Israel from the West, especially from the United States. It is of great importance that the early waves of immigration to Israel came from Eastern Europe, where these reforming movements—whose origins were in Western and Central Europe—had not penetrated. By contrast to American Jews, the Israeli community did not divide into different religious groups but rather into religious and secular in the way that was prevalent in Eastern Europe.

During the first years of Israel's independence, masses of immigrants from North Africa and the Middle East arrived in Israel. They had not been exposed to the processes of secularization and modernization that deeply influenced European Jewry from the beginning of the period of Emancipation. After arriving in Israel, many of these immigrants, especially the young among them, tended to become far more lax in the observance of religious commandments. Nevertheless, even among these groups, their loyalty and identity were clearly focused on the Orthodox community, and no attempt was made to establish alternative religious frameworks. Indeed, among Eastern Jews the proportion of those who are "traditional" in observance is especially high. Moreover, they tend to distinguish less radically between "religious" and "secular" than do Ashkenazi Jews. In short, there is little upon which a non-Orthodox movement could base itself.

Data from survey research reinforce these conclusions. It appears from these surveys that the relative weight of non-Orthodox groups is very small; indeed, it becomes clear that a goodly part of the Israeli population has no knowledge of their existence at all. In 1968 Yehuda Ben Meir and Perry Kedem conducted a survey in which the following question was asked: "Is there, in your opinion, a legitimate place in Israel for the Conservative Movement?" Thirty-nine percent of the respondents answered that they did "not know what it was."[1] Twenty-eight percent said they did not know what the Reform Movement was. In a survey conducted in 1988 by the Institute for Applied Social Research for the Ministry of Religion, a question was asked in regard to the respondent's self-identification with one of the three religious groups—Orthodox, Conservative, and Reform: 76 percent did not identify themselves with any religious group; 12 percent identified with the Orthodox; 9 percent with Reform; and 3 percent with the Conservatives.[2] One cannot deduce from this data, nevertheless, the relative weight of Orthodoxy in Israel because, as the survey's findings indicate, the terms used to describe religious self-definition

---

[1] These are unpublished results of a survey that Yehuda Ben-Meir and Perry Kedem conducted in 1968. Some of the survey results were reported in Yehuda Ben-Meir and Perry Kedem, "Index of Religiosity for the Jewish Population in Israel," *Megamot* (Hebrew) 24:3 (1979): 353–62.

[2] Hanna Levinson, *Public Positions and Evaluations on the Issues of Religion, Judaism, and the Institutions Designated to Deal with These Matters* (Jerusalem: Israel Institute of Applied Social Research, 1988, in Hebrew).

in Israel have little resonance for the greater part of the Israeli public.[3] This can be clearly seen in the fact that 31 percent of those who reported "observing all the religious commandments" and 85 percent of those who reported "observing most of the religious commandments" did not define themselves as Orthodox—although, typically, almost all of those in the first group and half of those in the second group defined themselves as "religious."

PATTERNS OF RELIGIOUS ORGANIZATION AND BEHAVIOR IN ISRAELI AND DIASPORA ORTHODOXY

The differences between Israel and the West are also apparent in the characteristics that are employed to determine belonging to "Orthodoxy," or, the "religious camp." While organizational loyalties are an important factor in determining one's belonging to Orthodoxy in the West, in Israel, allegiance to the religious camp is determined almost exclusively by one's religious behavior, by the degree of one's observance of the religious commandments. This carries great importance in regard to defining the limits of those included in "Orthodoxy."

In this regard it should be noted that the phenomena associated with "traditional" Judaism are not exclusive to Israel. In the United States and to an even greater degree in Western Europe, there are many Jews who do not observe a large part of the religious commandments. Nevertheless, they choose Orthodoxy as the context of their institutional loyalty. Interestingly, these Jews are regularly counted as Orthodox, while in Israel they would not be included in the "religious camp" either by themselves or by others.

The fact that one cannot really speak of "traditional" Jews as a special social category in the United States and in Western Europe

---

[3]Chaim Waxman correctly argues that "in Israel . . . the predominant conception of religion is quite different from that of the West, and religiosity is perceived much more in terms of observance." Chaim I. Waxman, "Orthodox Judaism in Israel," *Midstream* 37:9 (December 1991): 25.

does not essentially derive from their being only a small minority by comparison to their relative prevalence in Israel. The main reason relates to the self-definition of these Jews as part of the Orthodox community. Many of the observant Orthodox react to this self-definition more or less positively—or at least tolerantly. There are, to be sure, others within Orthodoxy who are unwilling to accept their self-styled Orthodoxy, and this has proved to be one of the main sources of cleavage within Diaspora Orthodoxy. All this means that the criteria by which the borders of membership in Diaspora Orthodoxy are delineated are broader and more inclusive than those that define the "religious camp" in Israel. This, of course, is of great importance in any comparison between Orthodox Jews in Israel and those in the Diaspora. A great many of those Jews who are counted "Orthodox" in the United States and West Europe would not be defined as "religious" in Israel.

In their research on Orthodoxy in the United States, Samuel Heilman and Steven Cohen distinguish between three types of Orthodox Jews. They are differentiated from each other by their religious behavior as well as by the totality of their religious, social, and political values.[4] The three categories are the "nominally Orthodox," the "Orthodox of the center," and the "traditionally Orthodox." In practice, the great majority of the "nominally Orthodox" as well as a small part of the "Orthodox of the center" would be defined as "traditional" in Israel. This conclusion can be reenforced by comparing the findings of Heilman and Cohen with the data provided by roughly parallel surveys conducted in Israel. Heilman and Cohen describe as "nominally Orthodox" those Jews who belong to an Orthodox synagogue and define themselves as "Orthodox"—even though they do not actively observe the religious commandments. Only 18 percent of the "nominally Orthodox" refrain from turning on lights on the Sabbath.[5] Only 34 percent report not viewing television on the Sab-

---

[4]Samuel C. Heilman and Steven M. Cohen, *Cosmopolitans and Parochials: Modern Orthodox Jews in America* (Chicago: University of Chicago Press, 1989), 41.

[5]Ibid., 60.

bath. Among the men included in this group, 59 percent go to synagogue every Sabbath, while only 31 percent report fasting on the Ninth of Ab. By contrast, the great majority of the "Orthodox of the center" observe these practices although, even among their numbers, there are about 8 percent who do not refrain from turning on lights and viewing television on the Sabbath, 7 percent who do not go to synagogue every Sabbath, and 5 percent who do not fast on the Ninth of Ab.

A different picture emerges from the findings of surveys conducted in Israel. Here, the proportion of Israeli Jews who define themselves as "religious" is lower than the proportion of those who perform a great many of the religious commandments. Among these commandments are included many that were not observed by the "nominally Orthodox" (and a small part of the "Orthodox of the center") in the United States. In the survey of Ben Meir and Kedem (1968) only 17 percent of the national cross-section that were questioned defined themselves as "religious," while 41 percent defined themselves as "traditional," and 42 percent characterized themselves as "secular."[6] Twenty-two percent of the resondents reported that they pray in a synagogue at least on the Sabbath, some 20 percent do not turn on electric appliances on the Sabbath. A similar proportion reported never turning on a radio on the Sabbath, and 18 percent reported that they "always" (14.5) or "usually" fast on the Ninth of Ab. Because the question was addressed to women as well as men it can be surmised that among the men the proportion of fasters was higher. (Only 78 percent of the women belonging to the "Orthodoxy of the center" in the Heilman-Cohen survey fasted on the Ninth of Ab as contrasted with 95 percent of the men.)

In a survey conducted in Israel during 1988 by the Institute for Applied Social Research,[7] 20 percent of the respondents defined themselves as "religious," 41 percent as "traditional" and 37 percent as "secular." Ten percent of the questioned said they "observe all the commandments," 18 percent "observe most of the commandments," 40 percent "observe some of the commandments," while 32 percent report that

[6]Ben-Meir and Kedem, "Index of Religiosity," 358.
[7]Levinson, *Public Positions*, 11.

they "do not observe any of the commandments." Those who define themselves as "religious Jews" constitute 92 percent of those who reported that they "observe all the commandments," 41 percent of those who "observe most of the commandments," and 8 percent of the rest.

The above findings verify the assertion that the main, almost exclusive criterion for self-definition as "religious" in Israel is the degree of religious observance. This contrasts with the importance of organizational membership as a criterion in the Diaspora. In the United States and even more so in the Western European countries, there is a sizable proportion of nonobservant Jews among those who define themselves as Orthodox in organizational terms. The explanation for this lies in the institutional preeminence of Orthodoxy among the Jewish communities of England and France. Non-Orthodox movements have failed in penetrating deeply into these states, despite the fact that observant Jews constitute only a minority within the Jewish community. It would seem then that Western Europe is, in this regard, closer to Israel than to the United States. Like the United States and in contrast to Israel, however, many Jews in these countries feel the need to express their Jewish identity by organizational membership in a religious community whose focus is the synagogue. While most institutionally affiliated American Jews belong to Conservative or Reform synagogues, in England and France they persist in belonging to Orthodox communities even when they are nonobservant. In Israel, by contrast, there is no real equivalent to "synagogue membership" as a communal framework, in the American and Western European sense. Neither does it have any substantial influence on Jewishness as an ethnocultural grouping or as a religious tradition. Once again the survey research findings verify these conclusions by demonstrating that the organizational-communal factor has only slight relevance for one's Jewish self-definition in Israel. While 17 percent of the respondents in the Ben Meir and Kedem survey defined themselves as "religious," only 5 percent reported that they belonged to "any religious organizations, associations or clubs."[8]

---

[8]These are unpublished results of the Ben-Meir and Kedem survey.

These differences in self-definition and communal belonging
are also of substantial relevance for intra-communal organization
and for the internal relationships that mark the Orthodox community. The presence of quite a large number of Jews who are not observant in the Diaspora Orthodox communities, especially in Western
Europe, is among the main reasons for the organization of the extremely observant in separate institutional frameworks that are
entirely independent of "official" Orthodoxy. These separate organizations have increased the relative importance of the "nominally
Orthodox" within the official Orthodox community, which, in turn,
only intensifies the tendency of the extremely observant to join the
separatist communities. This is one of the reasons that membership
in these separate communities is not limited to the non-Zionist "traditionally Orthodox" who broadly parallel the *haredi* (ultra-Orthodox) in Israel. For example, one can find in the separate Orthodox
community in Britain, Adas Yisroel, a considerable number of adherents who are positively disposed to modern culture and to Zionism.
These Jews found it hard to adjust to the official Orthodox communities affiliated to the United Synagogue—the majority of whose members are nonobservant. In contrast to England, one cannot speak of
an "official" Jewish community in the United States. Because pluralism is the central characteristic of American Judaism, there is no real
significance in the American context to a "schismatic" or separatist
community. What nevertheless unites American and Western European Orthodoxy is the absence of a common organizational base for
the various shades of Orthodoxy that differ from each other ideologi-
cally and socially.

In contrast to the Jewish communities in the Diaspora, in Israel
there does exist an organization in which all the main sectors of
Orthodoxy (or "religious Judaism") are represented, despite the major
social and ideological differences between them. These common
frameworks are the state-run religious institutions—the religious
councils, the rabbinate, and the rabbinical courts. To be sure, at their
inception these institutions were confronted by vigorous resistance
from the ultra-Orthodox circles associated with Agudat Israel. In-

deed, these circles continue to express reservations from the "official" religious establishment. The religious authorities they recognize are the roshei yeshivah (leaders of the yeshivah world) and the hasidic masters who are considered the great Torah authorities among the ultra-Orthodox public. Nevertheless, the haredim do, in fact, actively participate in the religious councils, and many of the rabbis and dayanim are from their ranks.[9] On the communal-organizational level only the most extreme ultra-Orthodox of the edah ha-haredit (the Community of the God-fearing) and the Neturei Karta (Guardians of the City) persist in their total separatism.

There are, of course, salient differences between the various elements within the religious camp in Israel, and in some important areas they are even more important than the differences that prevail between the different factions of Orthodoxy in the West.[10] Nevertheless, the existence of common religious and political frameworks is one of the factors that explains the cooperation between the various factions of Israeli Orthodoxy despite the important differences that divide them. In fact, this cooperation is more pronounced within Israeli Orthodoxy than in the Orthodox communities of the West.

At this point it is appropriate to assess the main criteria according to which distinctions are drawn between the various types of Orthodoxy in Israel and the West. The degree of observance is, as we have noted, the primary standard that Heilman and Cohen use to distinguish between the three types of Orthodoxy in the United States. These researchers conclude, however, that there exists among their respondents a correlation between the patterns of religious behavior, on the one hand, and their behavior patterns and beliefs in

---

[9]See Eliezer Don-Yehiya, *Religious Institutions in the Political System: The Religious Councils in Israel* (Jerusalem: The Jerusalem Center for Public Affairs, 1988, in Hebrew).

[10]The very fact that religious Zionists in Israel serve in the army, while the great majority of the *haredim* avoid any form of military service, is a significant distinguishing mark between the two sub-groups of Jewish Orthodoxy, which is unique to Israel.

regard to social, cultural, and political questions, on the other. Other students of American Jewry prefer using different terms to distinguish between the various types of American Orthodoxy. Charles Liebman speaks of "right-wing Orthodoxy" as opposed to "left-wing Orthodoxy" or "Modern Orthodoxy."[11] In his study of the world of the *yeshivah* in the United States, William Helmreich distinguishes between three types of observant American Orthodoxy: "Modern Orthodox," "Strictly Orthodox," and "Ultra-Orthodox."[12] The relevant question for us is, To what degree are these categories parallel to the distinctions between the various groups within the religious camp in Israel?

This is an especially critical question because from a number of perspectives the differences between Orthodoxy in Israel and Orthodoxy in the West are less pronounced than the intra-communal differences between the various groups constituting Orthodoxy in either Israel or the West. This renders it difficult to compare these intra-communal factions with each other without, at the same time, comparing them to their parallel factions in either Israel or the Diaspora. As becomes clear in Heilman and Cohen's research, the two types of "observant Orthodoxy" in the United States—"Orthodoxy of the center" and "traditional Orthodoxy"—are distinguished from each other according to the different levels of rigorous observance as well as their attitudes toward modernization. These criteria are also the basis of Helmreich's distinction between the "Modern" and the "Strictly" Orthodox and for Liebman's discrimination between "right-wing" and "left-wing" Orthodoxy.

By contrast, the most accepted distinction between the groups constituting the religious camp is that between the "national religious" (sometimes referred to simply as the "religious") and the "ultra-Orthodox" who are usually referred to as *haredim*. This distinction is

---

[11]Charles S. Liebman, "Modern Orthodoxy Today," *Midstream* 25:7 (August/September 1979): 19–26.

[12]William Helmreich, *The World of the Yeshiva* (New Haven: Yale University Press, 1982), 52.

based on their attitudes toward Zionism and the State of Israel rather than on the degree of rigor in the observance of the religious commandments. This is linked to the fact that, in contrast to what prevails in the Diaspora communities, Israeli Jews who do not observe the religious commandments place themselves outside the operative criterion for belonging to the religious community. There is, to be sure, a considerable degree of correlation between belonging to the "ultra-Orthodox" community, the tendency to be extremely rigorous in the observance of the religious commandments, and the rejection of the social and cultural implications of the modern world. Nevertheless, it is the relationship to Zionism and the State of Israel and not necessarily the degree of rigorous observance or even the rejection of modernity that is the primary criterion for distinguishing between the "ultra-Orthodox" and the other groups that belong to the religious camp in Israel.

THE RISE OF ORTHODOXY IN ISRAEL AND IN THE DIASPORA

An important development in the religious community in Israel, one that sharpens the distinction between Orthodoxy in Israel and the West, must be adverted to at this point. I refer to a deviation of the religious Zionist community from the basic traits that characterized it during the *Yishuv* and early statehood periods. Although the leaders and spokesmen of this community proclaimed their unconditional loyalty to the religious tradition, the exposure to Western modern culture was bound up with nonobservance of certain religious laws or traditional customs that were difficult to accommodate to modernity. Nevertheless, the most pronounced characteristic of this group is not adaptation so much as compartmentalization.[13] This approach manifests itself in the tendency to distinguish, in practice, between behav-

---

[13]On the distinction between various types of response to modernization within the Orthodox community, see Charles S. Liebman and Eliezer Don-Yehiya, *Civil Religion in Israel: Traditional Judaism and Political Culture*

ior that is *directed* by Jewish law and religious tradition and those other areas of personal and social life that are directed by considerations that do not clash with religious authority, but do not derive from this authority either. Even among those groups that continued to observe the religious commandments, there was a decrease in the centrality of religious values; they lost their controlling and exclusive role as the arbiter of behavior in all areas of life. In this regard there is much in common between the religious Zionists of the Yishuv period and the broad circles of the "Modern Orthodox" in America today.

To be sure, one can point to symptoms of a "religious resurgence," that is, a greater commitment to rigorous observation of religious commandments, in the American[14] as well as in other Diaspora Orthodox communities. In Britain, for example, researchers indicate that there is growing care in the observance of religious commandments among those who belong to "mainstream Orthodoxy" of the United Synagogue. This tendency to "religious resurgence" is expressed at the organizational-communal level as well: there is growing importance to the separatist Orthodox community, Adas Yisroel, at the expense of the established community of the United Synagogue.[15] A parallel development has taken place in the Jewish community in Australia.[16] These developments are usually not linked to a rise in the proportion of the Orthodox among the total Jewish population in the

---

in the Jewish State (Berkeley and Los Angeles: University of California Press, 1984), 185–204.

[14]Chaim I. Waxman, *America's Jews in Transition* (Philadelphia: Temple University Press, 1983), 124–28; Heilman and Cohen, *Cosmopolitans and Parochials*, 193–99; Charles S. Liebman and Steven M. Cohen, *Two Worlds of Judaism* (New Haven: Yale University Press, 1990), 126.

[15]Barry A. Kosmin and Caren Levi, *Synagogue Membership in the United Kingdom, 1983* (London: Research Unit Board of British Jews, 1983), 37–38; Ernest Krausz, "A Statistical Portrait of the Jewish Community in England," *Tfutzot Israel* (in Hebrew), 21:4 (1983): 57.

[16]Daniel Elazar with Peter Medding, *Jewish Communities in Frontier Societies* (New York: Holmes and Meier, 1983), 294–95, 306–09.

Diaspora—or, for that matter, in Israel. In essence, what has occurred is an inner strengthening of Orthodoxy as well as an arresting of the tendency to "abandon the fold" that, in the past, so sorely injured Orthodoxy and reduced its numbers, especially among the younger age groups and the older established cohorts.

One can, therefore, point to a convincing parallel between the dynamics of Orthodoxy in the Diaspora and in Israel that is expressed in the tendency of recovery and revival after a long period of decline and crisis. There is also a substantial similarity between factors that influenced the transformational process in Israel and in the Diaspora communities. Among these factors, a central role was played by developments in education that became manifest in the growth and broadening of "total," or "integral," religious educational networks. In the Western states, the growing scale and quality of Jewish day schools—largely Orthodox in character—stands out especially.[17] In the United States there is also a parallel growth in the network of upper-level *yeshivot* of the traditional kind. In Israel the most pronounced tendency is the development and spread of many varieties of *yeshivah* systems. On the one hand, there are the *yeshivot* of the traditional kind that have become the focal point of the ultra-Orthodox community. On the other, there is an accelerated growth

---

[17]Waxman, *America's Jews in Transition*, 125–26. In the United States, as in other Western countries, the resurgence of Jewish Orthodoxy was enhanced by the immigration of many Orthodox Jews from Eastern Europe, especially in the years prior to and after World War II (ibid., 124). As we have noted, observant Jews from Islamic countries formed a large portion of the mass immigration that arrived in Israel during its first years of independence. However, as many of the newcomers could not resist the influences of the secular Israeli society, this immigration was not a major factor in the resurgence of Orthodoxy in Israel. Furthermore, unlike immigrant spiritual leaders from Eastern Europe, who played a significant role in the revival of American Orthdoxy, the traditional leaders who immigrated to Israel from Islamic countries were not in a position to exert considerable influence on Israeli Orthodoxy. (In recent years there are, however, signs of religious revival in certain circles of sephardic Jews in Israel.)

and broadening in the network of high-school level and upper-level *yeshivot* of a novel kind that include many of the youth of the national religious community.[18]

One can also find parallels in the factors that initiated and energized the development of more "total" and "integrated" educational frameworks in Israel and in the West, especially the United States. It was precisely the failure of the "conventional" religious educational frameworks to retain their students within the religious fold that initiated and accelerated the efforts to arrest the dangerous "erosion." This was done by investing great energies in the cultivation of educational frameworks aimed at preserving the continuity and the integrality of the sacred values and the traditional ways of life.

From the beginning there were, nevertheless, differences between the character and scope of these educational developments in Israel and Western states. These variations reflected the dissimilarity in the starting points from which the two developments originated. In the Jewish communities of the Diaspora, the transformation was expressed in a move from the "partial" frameworks of Jewish-religious education, to the integral day-school framework. In Israel, by contrast, the transformation took place, in large measure, at the expense of the conventional religious high schools. Parallel to this development there was a great broadening of the traditional *yeshivot* and the nationalist *yeshivot* of the new type—the *yeshivot hesder* (*yeshivot* that combine higher religious study with army service) and Mercaz Harav and its affiliates.

In the United States as well there was a growth of upper-level *yeshivot* of the traditional kind, but the development of *yeshivot* in Israel has been far more accelerated than in the United States. The most important point in this regard is that the network of upper-level *yeshivot* in the United States is aimed especially at the circles of

---

[18]Eliezer Don-Yehiya, "The Book and the Sword: The Nationalist Yeshivot and Political Radicalism in Israel," in *Accounting for Fundamentalism: The Dynamic Character of Fundamentalist Movements*, ed. Martin Marty and R. Scott Appleby (Chicago: University of Chicago Press, in press).

"right-wing Orthodoxy," while most of the "modern Orthodox" are satisfied with the education given in the framework of the day schools. The only upper-level *yeshivah* that draws from among modern Orthodox circles is Yeshiva University. Notably, this institution combines within its framework secular studies alongside religious studies and is, in this regard, different not only from the traditional *yeshivot* but also from the nationalist *yeshivot* in Israel. In contrast to the United States, the Israeli traditional *yeshivah* education that is characterized by exclusive concentration on religious studies, especially Talmud, is no longer the exclusive domain of the "ultra-Orthodox." Rather, there are broader and larger constituencies from among the national religious camp that are part of this educational pattern. The differences in this regard are related to an additional characteristic of special importance that distinguishes the process of religious change in Israel from that in the Western states. In contrast to these latter communities, the process of religious resurgence in Israel is tied to and inextricable from a move toward national-political extremism. It is to this subject that we now turn.

THE MOVE TOWARD "RELIGIOPOLITICAL EXTREMISM" IN ISRAELI SOCIETY

Prior to the establishment of the State of Israel and in the early years of its existence, Orthodox Jewry in Israel and the Diaspora was characterized by moderate political positions. This moderation was common to the different varieties of Orthodoxy—from the ultra-Orthodox to the Zionist. Its source, was, to be sure, quite different in the two camps. Among ultra-Orthodox Jewry, this moderate position was based on the passive approach of traditional Judaism, which stood in strict opposition to the activist political stance that characterized Zionism as a movement for national liberation. In opposition to the ultra-Orthodox, the Zionists attempted to adapt the Jewish religious tradition to the political activism of Zionism. However, under the influence of and exposure to the universalist values of Western culture, most religious Zionists were opposed to extreme nationalist positions. The impression was created, therefore, that religiosity and political moderation were mutually reinforcing.

Against this background, the turnabout in perceptions regarding the relationship between religiosity and political radicalism in Israel is quite dramatic. The religious tradition, which was previously understood as a source of passivity or political moderation, is broadly perceived in contemporary Israeli society as a factor that encourages radical nationalism and extremist political activism. This perception was especially strengthened by the support for radical nationalist positions among many strictly observant Jews who evinced an uncompromising dedication to Jewish law and strove for its application to all areas of life. The relevant question therefore is, What were the factors that led to this blending of radicalism in both the religious and political domains? This is for us an especially intriguing question because this phenomenon is quite unique to the religious community in Israel and distinguishes it from the Orthodox communities in the Diaspora.

In large measure, this stems from the establishment and striking growth of educational networks that combine traditional *yeshivah* studies with an affirmative attitude to Zionism and the Jewish state as well as encouraging a positive disposition toward Israeli society in general.

This is a novel phenomenon, as traditional *yeshivot* used to constitute a fortress of opposition to Zionism since its early origins. To be sure, there were attempts on the part of the religious Zionists to establish *yeshivot* with a positive attitude to Zionism and a greater openness to general culture. Nevertheless, these attempts were not very successful during the *Yishuv* and early statehood period. The ultra-Orthodox non-Zionist *yeshivot* continued to play the central role in Torah education in Israel as well as in the Diaspora. In large measure, this can be explained by the very nature of the *yeshivah* as an educational institution. It is difficult to accommodate the traditional *yeshivah* to the adaptationist attitudes that prevailed in the religious-Zionist camp in regard to modern society and culture. The children and youth from religious-Zionist homes were, therefore, very largely educated in elementary schools, high schools, and teachers' seminars in which secular studies constituted the larger part of the curriculum and in which the religious atmosphere that prevailed was quite luke-warm in character. A number of Zionist *yeshivot* were, in fact, estab-lished during the pre-state period, but their numbers were very small and they were limited to the high-school level. The upper-level *yeshivot* that represent the goal of *yeshivah* study continued to belong almost entirely to the traditional ultra-Orthodox type.

Prior to the establishment of the state, the single upper-level *yeshivah* in Israel that deviated from this pattern and educated its stu-dents to identify with the Zionist enterprise and to openness toward the general Jewish community was the Mercaz Harav *yeshivah*. This *yeshivah* was founded by Rabbi Avraham Yitzhak Kook, the first chief rabbi in the Land of Israel, who is considered one of the most original and admired Jewish thinkers of the modern period. At a later stage, after the establishment of the state and the Six Day War, Mercaz Harav became the main source of inspiration for the awakening of an activist messianism in the religious-Zionist community. It also served as the reservoir out of which the central leaders and activists of the Gush Emunim movement were originally recruited.

After the Six Day War, a process of accelerated growth and devel-opment of upper-level *yeshivot* began within the religious-Zionist camp. The growth of a network of high-level nationalist *yeshivot* was en-couraged by a development, the first signs of which preceded the pe-riod of statehood. This was the establishment and expansion of a net-work of "high-school *yeshivot*," the students of which came from religious-Zionist homes and whose curriculum combined secular stud-ies with intensive religious learning.[19] In large measure, the establish-ment of the high-school *yeshivot* can be attributed to the penetration of secularizing tendencies into the religious-Zionist public, many of whose young abandoned the religious way of life—to the dismay of

---

[19]Mordechai Bar-Lev, *The Graduates of the Yeshiva High School in Eretz-Yisrael: Between Tradition and Innovation* (Ph.D. diss., Bar-Ilan University, 1977, in Hebrew).

their parents and teachers. The sense of failure and impotence that prevailed in the religious educational network was an important motivating force in the efforts to establish educational institutions in which the identification with Zionism and the state would be at one with the preservation of the integral religious worldview and way of life.

The great expansion of the nationalist *yeshivah* network at the high school and upper level was central in the growing influence of a new religious and national outlook. This outlook is unique to the religious-Zionist public in Israel and differentiates it from other religious or modern Orthodox groups in the United States and other Jewish communities in Diaspora. The source of this outlook is in the Mercaz Harav *yeshivah* that played a key role in the religious and political life of post–Six Day War Israel. "Mercaz Harav" was dedicated to the realization of the religious and social ideals of its founder, Rabbi Kook, as well as to their presentation as an inspirational model for the Jewish community at large. This system of ideas as well as the educational framework that was founded to cultivate them represent a singular kind of response to modernization and secularization as well as to the Zionist awakening.[20] This model is quite sharply distinct from either the ultra-Orthodox response or the classic religious-Zionist response that continue to be accepted in the various sectors of Diaspora Jewry. The emphasis in this approach on the centrality of religion and the uncompromising stand in regard to the integrality of Jewish values and its way of life are, in fact, closer to the ultra-Orthodox approach than to the conventional position of the religious Zionists.

Nevertheless, the centrality of religion in Rabbi Kook's approach and his uncompromising devotion to religious principles are linked neither to a strategy of isolation and defensiveness in regard to modern society at large nor to a policy of passivity and nonengagement with sociopolitical life. On the contrary, it was precisely the insistence on the centrality of religion that made it imperative in his view

---

[20]Eliezer Don-Yehiya, "Jewish Orthodoxy, Zionism, and the State of Israel," *The Jerusalem Quarterly* 31 (1984): 10–29.

to make every effort to rescue it from the narrow domain it occupied in the Diaspora and to extend its influence to all areas of individual and social life. To this end, it was imperative in this view to undertake an activist program in the religious and sociopolitical realms as well as to reach out a brotherly hand to circles that stood outside the religious community.

Perhaps the clearest expression of this "expansionist" approach is to be found in the relationship of Rabbi Kook and his disciples to the Zionist movement and to the secular Jews who directed it. To be sure, Rabbi Kook was vigorously opposed to the symptoms of secularization that marked the Zionist movement. And yet, he attributed a sacred status to Jewish nationalism and to the Zionist enterprise. It was, in his eyes, an expression of religious renewal and a national renaissance that signals the beginning of the messianic redemption.

It should be noted, however, that even Rabbi Avraham Yitzhak Kook's teachings do not explicitly justify political radicalism in the name of the messianic idea.[21] The source of this idea is, in fact, in the teachings of Rabbi Kook's son, Rabbi Tzvi Yehudah, who, for a long period was the head of Mercaz Harav and became the spiritual leader of the *Gush Emunim* movement. The novelty of Rabbi Tzvi Yehudah and his students' ideas lies in the radical interpretation they give to the messianic idea. This radicalism sees messianism not only as an object to be pursued but also as an idea that justifies the means used in its pursuit. In this approach not only the objectives but also the programs and the ways of acting are defined in messianic terms. Therefore, they too are placed outside the limits and constraints imposed by mundane reality. Notably, this includes the need to take into account policies and interests of other nations as well as the pressures that they may exert.

This outlook is closely related to the distinction between periods of exile and periods of redemption that are distinguished from

---

[21]Eliezer Don-Yehiya, "Jewish Messianism, Religious Zionism, and Israeli Politics: The Impact and Origins of Gush Emunim," *Middle Eastern Studies* 23:2 (1987): 215–34.

one another in the sharpest terms. Religious Zionism, in all its varieties, accepts the argument that passivity is not an integral part of the
Jewish tradition but rather is rooted in the existential conditions of
the Diaspora. Therefore, the Jewish people must liberate itself from
this attitude in the process of its return to the Land of Israel and the
renewal of its political independence. This argument is central to the
political activism of religious Zionism, while the passive attitude of
the ultra-Orthodox rests on the opposite assumption: that the People
of Israel continues to find itself in Exile even after the establishment
of the state.[22] Nevertheless, classic religious Zionism does not accept
the view that the period of Redemption allows, even mandates, a
radical transformation in sociopolitical patterns of behavior. This
radical view, by contrast, gained a foothold in the outlooks of those
circles associated with Mercaz Harav and other *yeshivot* of its type.
Under the influence of Rabbi Tzvi Yehudah Kook, they strongly insist
that any retreat from territories occupied by Israel is tantamount to
sabotaging the process of messianic redemption.

The radical messianism of these circles is one reason that they
take militant positions in regard to political and security issues. But
this militancy reflects an interesting blend of a particularist approach
whose source lies in traditional Judaism, and a national-political
activism the main source of which lies in modern Zionism.

This synthesis of traditional Jewish particularism and modern
political activism differs, on the one hand, from the traditional *haredi*
approach. The *haredi* position is one in which separatist and hostile
attitudes toward non-Jews are mitigated by a passive approach that
disqualifies any exercise of political power in relations to Gentiles.
On the other hand, the particularist-activist stance differs from that
of classical religious Zionism, which, while accepting the political
activism of modern Zionism, reflected the influence of universalist

---

[22]Aviezer Ravitzky, "Exile in the Holy Land: The Dilemma of Haredi
Jewry," in *Israel: State and Society, 1948–1988*, Studies in Contemporary
Jewry, vol. 5, ed. Peter Medding (New York: Oxford University Press,
1989), 89–125.

values that prevailed in that movement, especially in its socialist wing.

These universalist tendencies have been greatly weakened within Israeli society in general and the religious community in particular. This was caused by events such as the Holocaust, Israeli wars with its Arab neighbors, the growing isolation of Israel in the international arena after the Six Day War, and the decline of Zionist socialism and *mamlakhtiut* (statism). Within the ranks of the religious Zionist public in Israel, these developments reflect the impact of the teachings of Rav Tzvi Yehudah Kook, which represent a fusion of rigorous halakhic religiosity with a radical messianic nationalism of an extreme particularist and activist kind. The great expansion of the nationalist *yeshivot* inspired by Mercaz Harav further enhanced the acceptance of this approach in broad circles of the Israeli religious community.

PARTICULARISM AND UNIVERSALISM AMONG THE ORTHODOX IN ISRAEL AND THE DIASPORA

This approach is not characteristic of all those who count themselves part of the religious Zionist camp. There are even those who dissociate themselves from it within the world of the nationalist *yeshivot*. To one degree or another, however, the Mercaz Harav–centered view is a prevailing influence in the religious Zionist camp and, at times, even outside its confines. Herein lies one of the most outstanding differences between contemporary Jewish Orthodoxy in Israel and in the Diaspora. To be sure, one can identify processes of religious resurgence in Diaspora Orthodoxy. Nevertheless, these processes are not generally combined with parallel tendencies to national and political radicalization. This can be associated with a number of factors that, in turn, reflect the differences between the values and outlooks of Israeli and Western Orthodoxy. First of all, in contrast to its influence in Israel, the radical conception of messianism has not struck root among Diaspora Jewry. The idea of the Jewish state as the beginning of the Redemption is, to be sure, broadly accepted among the religious Zionists and the modern Orthodox; nevertheless, this conception does not generally entail support for the national-political radicalism of Mercaz Harav and Gush Emunim.[23]

In large measure this can be accounted for by the existential conditions of Diaspora Jews that make it difficult for them to identify with a "messianism of the here and now," that is, by its very nature, tied to a rejection of Diaspora Jewish life. In this context, it should be noted that the "rejection of the Diaspora," which was a central tenet of secular Zionism, finds its greatest support in contemporary Israel in the religious Zionist camp and especially in those circles associated with Gush Emunim and the nationalist *yeshivot*.[24] The great emphasis that this outlook places on the necessity for a total break of the Jewish people with the Exile and an end to contacts with it finds symptomatic expression in the opposition that is often voiced to foreign travel.

As can be surmised from the above, the relationship of these circles to the Diaspora is anchored in the teachings of Rabbi Tzvi Yehudah Kook, for whom a radical rejection of the Diaspora is utterly basic. There is a clear tie between the particularist elements in Rabbi Kook's teachings and his rejection of the Diaspora. The Diaspora

---

[23]Admittedly, certain circles of American Orthodox Jews tend to combine particularist tendencies with activist, even aggressive, attitudes toward non-Jews. (A case in point are many of the writers published in *The Jewish Press*.) However, their position in American Orthodoxy is rather marginal in comparision to the position of their counterparts in Israeli Orthodoxy. Furthermore, most of the militant elements within American Orthodoxy do not tend to present an elaborate and all-embracing religious-nationalist ideology of the kind that is so influential within the religious Zionist community in Israel.

[24]Eliezer Don-Yehiya, "Galut in Zionist Ideology and in Israeli Society," in *Israel and Diaspora Jewry: Ideological and Political Persectives*, ed. E. Don-Yehiya (Ramat-Gan: Bar-Ilan University Press, 1991), 221–57, especially 242–43.

represents for him the "world of the nations"—an extremely alien and hostile world from which Jews must rescue themselves by any and all means and return to their homeland. In his view, the Holocaust signifies the total uprooting of the Jews from the Diaspora and its severing of all ties with the world of non-Jews. The unspeakable catastrophe of the Jewish people only affirms that the only place for the nation of Israel and its Torah is in the Land of Israel. The establishment of the Jewish state, which secular Zionists understood as a return of Israel to the family of nations, was perceived by the messianic religious Zionists as the segregation of the Jewish people into a separate and singular cultural political framework.

This outlook was expressed in a political position that combines the rejection of the Diaspora with an uncompromising insistence on "the greater Land of Israel." The emphatic opposition between Israel and the nations leads to a rejection of Jewish existence in Diaspora and to the conclusion that one should not place any trust in other nations or states or, for that matter, take their positions into consideration, when Israeli interests are at stake. The rejection of the Diaspora as a condition of dependence and weakness also leads to a raising of the Israeli army and its weaponry to the level of a central value to be cultivated and made as powerful as possible. Similarly, the insistence on the singular and unconditional holiness of the Land of Israel and the State of Israel leads to the rejection of Diaspora existence that is cut off from the sources of holiness in the Land and in the State.

It is quite evident that Jews living in the Diaspora find it hard to identify with the "rejection of the Diaspora" as an operational principle—even though they define themselves as religious Zionists. In addition, the difference between the existential condition of Jews in the Diaspora and those in Israel makes it difficult for Orthodox Jews in the Diaspora to support the position of the Mercaz Harav. The political radicalism of this position was nourished by the combination of traditional particularism and modernist political activism. But while a truly particularist approach is readily integrated with a view that is isolationist in cultural and organization terms—such as that supported by Israeli particularists—it is more difficult to sustain in the pluralist and open societies of the West. This is especially true of those who are part of "Modern Orthodoxy" in the West. And yet there is also a significant difference in this regard between the ultra-Orthodox in Israel and ultra-Orthodox in the Diaspora. Prevailing conditions in Israeli society, especially its tendency to intensify particularist sentiments, underpin and encourage the traditional particularism in ultra-Orthodox circles. This stands in contrast to the Western states, in which even many of the ultra-Orthodox find it difficult to preserve attitudes and behavior patterns that are truly particularistic.

In Heilman and Cohen's research on American Orthodoxy, 70 percent of the "Orthodox of the center" and 44 percent of the "traditional Orthodox" expressed the opinion that "an Orthodox Jew can be in close ties of friendship with non-Jews."[25] According to the same survey, somewhat less than half (44 percent) of the "Orthodox of the center" and about two-thirds of the "traditional Orthodox" (67 percent) reported that they do not have close friends who are not Jewish. Although there has been no such polling among Orthodox Jews in Israel, the clear impression is that they show far lesser willingness to maintain friendships with non-Jews. An indication of this is found in a survey conducted by Yoav Peled, of the political science department of Tel Aviv University, close to the elections for the 12th Knesset in 1988.[26] In this survey, whose objective was to measure the degree of distance between Israeli Jews and Israeli Arabs, those questioned divided not according to their degree of religiosity but according to their party affiliations. The answers of those who supported the religious parties reflected a very great degree of social distance from Israeli Arabs. It is far greater than the distance reflected in the answers of the supporters of other parties (excepting Meir Kahane's Kach party). Practically all the voters for religious parties (93 percent) declared that they did not have a close Arab friend, 87 percent refrained from inviting Arabs home, and 83 percent did not

---

[25]Heilman and Cohen, *Cosmopolitans and Parochials*, 123.

[26]The survey results were presented by Yoav Peled in the annual meeting of the Israeli Political Science Association (Jerusalem, 1989).

even have "passing contacts" with them. The supporters of religious parties also tended heavily to adopt negative images of Arabs. Seventy-five percent perceived of Israeli Arabs as "Jew haters" and 76 percent charged that the Arabs "take work opportunities" away from Jews.

It can be argued of course that the symptoms of isolation characterizing Orthodox Israeli Jews are not directed toward non-Jews in general but rather, first and foremost, against Arabs. The source of this attitude, it may well be claimed, is in the hostility between Israel and the Arab states and the violence of the various Palestinian groups toward Israel. It needs to be emphasized, nevertheless, that the findings cited above focus on the relationship of religious party supporters to Israeli Arabs and that the former do not tend to discriminate almost at all between Israeli Arabs and those living in the territories. This contrasts to the supporters of other parties, including the Likud, that tend far more to make this distinction. Yoav Peled concludes therefrom that the attitude of the religious toward the Arabs reflects particularist tendencies toward non-Jews and not just a reaction to the manifestations of violence on the part of the Arabs.

A study of the literature and the publicist material of the religious camp in Israel strengthens the impression that there is a growing tendency to adopt clearly particularist positions in regard to the relations between Israel and the nations of the world. Although positions such as these are most pronounced in the Mercaz Harav school, their influence is also substantial among the broad ranks of the religious Zionists public as well as the ultra-Orthodox community. Israel's perilous position as a "state under siege" only serves to intensify these particularist sentiments.

The differences between Israeli and Diaspora Orthodoxy reflect, in large measure, the broader divisions between Israeli Jewry and Diaspora communities. These divisions are the subject of a study by Charles Liebman and Steven Cohen, who explore disparate approaches and values that characterize the Jewish communities of Israel and the United States. One of the most outstanding differences is the powerful tendency of American Jewry to adopt liberal and universalist attitudes that are strongly at odds with the particularist tendencies of

Israeli Jews. Liebman and Cohen note that this difference does not stem from the higher proportion of Orthodox Jews in Israel.[27] There are differences in this regard even between the Orthodox in Israel and in the United States. They conclude that these differences mainly reflect the different structural conditions of the two realities. They especially emphasize the very obvious fact that by contrast to American Jews, who are only a part of a general society the great majority of which is not Jewish, the Israeli society to which they belong is entirely Jewish.[28]

THE ATTITUDE TO MODERN CULTURE IN ISRAELI AND WESTERN ORTHODOXY

To this point the discussion has turned on attitudes of the Orthodox to non-Jewish society. Below we shall compare the positions of the Orthodox in Israel and in the West in regard to modern culture. It has been said that one can characterize the prevailing attitude in Western Orthodoxy as a compartmentalization between, on the one hand, the religious realm that is directed by the religious commandments, and, on the other, diverse areas of life that are influenced by the values and the reality of modern culture and society. According to Charles Liebman, "compartmentalization is especially appropriate to the conditions of the Diaspora in which the model of the dominant culture encourages the distinction between the religious identity of the individual and the attitude toward economic and political matters, including many social and cultural aspects of life."[29] By contrast, it is far harder to legitimate such a model in Israel because the general unwillingness "to define the society, the culture, and the political establishment of the Jewish State as irrelevant from a Jewish

---

[27]Liebman and Cohen, *Two Worlds of Judaism*, 164–65.

[28]Ibid., 166–71.

[29]Charles S. Liebman, "Religion and the Chaos of Modernity," in Jacob Neusner, *Take Judaism for Example* (Chicago: University of Chicago Press, 1983), 157.

point of view." Chaim Waxman also writes that compartmentalization is "the dominant reaction of American Orthodoxy to the problem of modernization and secularization."[30] He emphasizes that it is
impossible to apply Rabbi Kook's "integral" or "expansionist" model
to American Orthodoxy because this approach is predicated upon
the existence of a sovereign Jewish society in the framework of which
it is possible to imprint the religious seal on all areas of life. This
approach is, therefore, more appropriate to Israel. Indeed, Waxman
points out that one of the main reasons given by the American Orthodox for their immigration to Israel is the sense that in Israel "they will
be able to live a fuller and more complete Jewish life."[31] The question
that needs to be asked is what exactly does "expansionism" signify
and what are its concrete expressions. For our purposes, it is especially important to explore to what degree this approach encourages
a positive attitude toward modern culture. It is appropriate to recall
here that Rabbi Avraham Yitzhak Kook's approach intended to
broaden the influence of religion on all areas of life. In practice, however, it was expressed especially in the relationship to Jewish nationalism and the Zionist enterprise. This can be seen by comparing the
attitude to general education and culture in the theoretical writings
of Rabbi Kook and the actual place of general studies in his *yeshivah*,
Mercaz Harav. In his writings, Rabbi Kook expresses great admiration for the achievements of mankind in the realms of cultural creation and scientific research. Moreover, he relates positively to these
areas as ways of revealing the Divine light that is hidden in them.
Nevertheless, in his own *yeshivah*, Mercaz Harav, there was exclusive
concentration on the holy sources of Jewish religious tradition. At a
later stage, the tendency to isolation from so-called alien ideas and
foreign cultural influences grew stronger still.

The difference between the Mercaz Harav school and the ultra-
Orthodox *yeshivot* in Israel is, therefore, manifest specifically in re-

---

[30]Chaim I. Waxman, *American Aliya: Portrait of an Innovative Migration
Movement* (Detroit: Wayne State University Press, 1989), 133.

[31]Ibid., 134–35.

gard to Jewish nationalism and political activism. The isolationist outlook of the ultra-Orthodox is directed toward modern-secular society as a whole—whether Jewish or not. In this category are included Zionism and its politically active attitude. Both of these are perceived as standing in opposition to the spirit of Jewish tradition. They derive, so the ultra-Orthodox charge, from the alien source of modern secular nationalism, whose object is to blur the uniqueness of the Jewish nation and to transform it into a "nation like other nations." In the approach of the Mercaz Harav school as well there are manifestations of isolation from secular studies and modern culture. Nonetheless, this outlook does not apply to Zionism that is perceived, in the spirit of Rabbi Kook's teachings, as a sacred idea.

The distinction between attitudes to Zionism, secular Jewish society, and the Jewish state, on the one hand, and modern culture on the other can be applied to the ultra-Orthodox as well—but in a diametrically opposed way. While the greater part of those who oppose Zionism are also characterized by opposition to and isolation from modern culture, there are those whose negative attitude toward Zionism and secular Jewish society is bound up with an openness toward modern Western culture. The attitude of (what may be called) the "neo-Orthodox," whose main axis is in the teachings of Rabbi Samson Raphael Hirsch, can be understood as the antithesis of the Mercaz Harav outlook. By contrast to the views of some scholars, the difference between the outlooks of Rabbi Hirsch and of Rabbi Kook is not mainly focused on the divide between compartmentalization, which is ascribed to "neo-Orthodoxy," and the expansionist approach, which is associated with Rabbi Kook's school.[32] Both these approaches oppose the total isolationism of the ultra-Orthodox as well as the adaptationist policies of pre-statehood religious Zionism. The main difference between them is that the "openness" of the Mercaz Harav school is directed mainly toward Zionism and the

---

[32]According to Waxman, this is the view of Charles Liebman and Norman Lamm (ibid., 133). Liebman ascribes this view to Ismar Schorsh (Liebman, *Religion and the Chaos of Modernity*, 157).

State of Israel, while "neo-Orthodox" openness relates mainly to modern Western culture.

This point is especially relevant for a comparison between Orthodoxy in Israel and in the Western countries. One of the unique and characteristic qualities of the religious Jewish community in Israel— one that distinguishes it from the Diaspora Orthodoxy—is the growing influence achieved by the synthesis of religious resurgence and national-political radicalization. By contrast, Diaspora Orthodoxy is unique in the large proportions of those who combine great rigor in the observation of the religious commandments with a great degree of openness toward modern culture and education. The "enlightened ultra-Orthodox" in the spirit of Rabbi Samson Raphael Hirsch are, to be sure, a minority in Orthodox Western society. And yet, the approach that derives from Rabbi Hirsch—"Torah and worldliness"— is widely adopted by many Orthodox circles that are not part of neo-Orthodoxy. Similarly, even though the "nationalist ultra-Orthodox" in the spirit of the Rabbis Kook are also a minority among Israel's religious community, their ideas are influential in many broad circles that are not part of the nationally oriented *yeshivot* or Gush Emunim.

The differences in this area between Israeli and Diaspora Orthodoxy become clearly manifest in a comparison of the attitudes toward general education among Israeli and Western ultra-Orthodox. One of the salient characteristics of the Israeli ultra-Orthodox is their vigorous opposition to the integration of "secular studies" beyond the most elementary level of instruction. Virtually all study time is devoted to religious learning and especially to the study of *Gemara*. By contrast, general studies are incorporated in most of the ultra-Orthodox educational institutions in the West, apart from upper-level *yeshivot*.

The most important point is that with all of the great value that American ultra-Orthodoxy places on *yeshivah* study, the *yeshivah* does not constitute a global and total way of life. It is not uncommon for some among the ultra-Orthodox not to continue their studies in an upper-level *yeshivah*. Even those who do study in an upper-level *yeshivah* do not remain in it after marriage or beyond a specified period of study. By contrast, in Israel there has developed a unique and unparalleled phenomenon of a community of scholars—focused on the various ultra-Orthodox *yeshivot*—as a total way of life that is, in practice, obligatory for all men, both young and old.

The difference between the status of the *yeshivah* in ultra-Orthodox society in Israel and in the United States is also manifest to a degree in the nature of *yeshivah* education in the two contexts. To be sure, it is difficult to point to essential differences between the respective curricula and learning schedules of the Israeli and American *yeshivot*—both are based on the same "classical" model of the Lithuanian *yeshivah*. Nevertheless, despite the fact that isolation from the outside world is a common trait of all traditional *yeshivot*, the degree and severity of this isolation is usually far greater in the Israeli case. This disparity is manifest in their different approach to general education. In principle, the ultra-Orthodox *yeshivot* of the United States have their reservations about general or secular studies—most especially in regard to university education. In practice, however, they resign themselves to the prevalent tendency among *yeshivah* students to enroll for higher education in evening and summer courses.[33] The traditional ultra-Orthodox *yeshivot* in Israel, by contrast, vigorously resist any enrollment in university courses—they simply refuse to consider the possibility that a student would study in the *yeshivah* and in the university simultaneously. This uncompromising opposition to secular learning is the characteristic trait of the ultra-Orthodox in Israel as opposed to the more lenient, at times even silently positive, attitude of the traditional *yeshivot* in the United States.

In this area as well the differences between the Orthodox in Israel and in the Diaspora are tied to the structural conditions of the two societies. In this regard, two main points need to be made. First, there is the issue of funding. Only in Israel do the *yeshivot* enjoy generous government aid that permits the students to devote all their energies to study for long periods of time. Second, although there is a basic unwillingness to admit it expressly, it seems that the deferral from army service that is given to *yeshivah* students while they study is an incentive

---

[33]Helmreich, *The World of the Yeshiva*, 200.

for some of them to remain within the educational setting for very long periods of time. Whatever may be their motives, these features of Israeli life encourage and cultivate isolationist attitudes to the surrounding society. This stems from the very nature of the *yeshivah* as a total framework for intensive socialization. The Israeli ultra-Orthodox community, therefore, being a "community of *yeshivot*," tends, far more than do the ultra-Orthodox communities in the Diaspora, toward a rejection of and isolation from the culture of modern society.

On the other hand, despite the reservations that the ultra-Orthodox express in regard to Zionist ideology, there are signs that testify to their increasing engagement with Israeli society and politics. Although this process is directed above all by pragmatic considerations—chiefly the need to recruit funding for the ultra-Orthodox educational system—the very engagement itself tends to exert its influence on the positions the ultra-Orthodox adopt in practice. In opposition to most of the religious Zionists, the ultra-Orthodox in Israel do not ascribe religious or messianic significance to the state; nevertheless, they harbor a great deal of concern about its existence, peace, and welfare. Despite their criticism of the state, they feel themselves a part of it. The very fact that their surroundings are Israeli leads them to become attached to Israel far more than the Diaspora ultra-Orthodox.[34] In this regard as well then, the place does indeed make a difference.

---

[34]Daniel Gutenmacher, who has studied the attitude of Agudath Israel in America toward the State of Israel, concludes that "the politics of confrontation remains the dominant direction and atmosphere of the organization." He further argues that "in regard to the . . . issue of the relationship to Israel one can detect a certain difference between Agudist circles in the two countries [Israel and the United States]. Israel loses its centrality for American . . . Agudists in a way that probably only distance can explain." Daniel Gutenmacher, "Agudath Israel of America and the State of Israel: The Case of the Jewish Observer," in *Israel and Diaspora Jewry: Ideological and Political Perspectives*, ed. Eliezer Don-Yehiya (Ramat-Gan: Bar-Ilan University Press, 1991), 126.

3

The Obligation of *Aliyah* and the Prohibition of Leaving Israel in the Contemporary Era, According to the Opinion of Rambam (Maimonides)

Yoel Bin-Nun

Every learned Jew knows that, according to Ramban (Nahmanides) and his colleagues, there is a communal biblical *mitzvah* to conquer *Eretz Yisrael*, and in every generation, even during the period of Dispersion, for each individual to make *aliyah*. Many, however, rely on the opinion of Rambam, who did not enumerate this *mitzvah* in his *Sefer ha-Mitzvot*. In this chapter, I will attempt to elucidate the opinion of Rambam and the demands that derive from it, particularly in the contemporary era.

In the *Tosefta* of *Avodah Zarah*, chap. 5, the sages said:

"A man should live in *Eretz Yisrael*, even in a city where the majority are non-Jews and not abroad or in a city where *everyone is Jewish*." This teaches that the settlement of *Eretz Yisrael* is equivalent to all the *mitzvot* in the Torah, and whoever is buried in *Eretz Yisrael*, it is as if he were buried beneath the Altar.[1]

A man did not go outside the country unless wheat was selling at a rate of two *seahs* to the *sela*. Said Rabbi Simeon: this is only when there were no takers, but when there were, he did not go even when the rate was a *seah* to a *selah*. And so Rabbi Simeon would say: Elimelekh was among the great ones of the generation and a community leader; yet, for leaving Israel, he and his sons died while all of Israel survived on their own soil, as it is written: "All the city was astir at their arrival, and they said, 'Is this Naomi?'" (Ruth 1:19). This teaches that the whole city lived through the famine but that Elimelekh and his sons died of starvation.

For indeed, he [Jacob] says: "So that I come back to my father's house in peace," and there is no reason to say, "then the Lord shall be my God" (Genesis 28:21). And it is written: "I am the Lord your God who brought you out of the Land of Egypt to give you the Land of Canaan, to be your God" (Leviticus 25:38). So long as you are in the Land of Canaan I will be your God, but if you are not in the Land of Canaan, *one may say, I will not be your God*. So it is written: "And the children of Reuben, and the children of Gad, and half the tribe of Menashe, passed over armed before the children of Israel, as Moshe spoke to them. About forty thousand prepared for war passed over before the Lord to battle, to the plains of Jericho" (Joshua 4:12–13). Would it occur to us that Israel conquered the Land before the Omnipresent? No; but as long as they are upon it, it is as if it is conquered, but when they are not upon it, it is as if it is not conquered.

---

[1]In the text of the Babylonian Talmud, *Ketubbot* 110 b, and Rambam, Laws of Kings 5:12, it states, where the majority are Jewish.

And it is written: "for they have driven me out this day from being joined to the inheritance of the Lord, saying, Go, serve the gods" (1 Samuel 26:18). Would it occur to us that David was serving heathen gods? Rather, David spoke in parables and said: whosoever leaves the country *in peace-time* and goes to other lands [in the words of the Talmud, *Ketubbot* 110b: whoever lives abroad . . .] is like one who serves heathen gods.

As it is written: "Behold, I will gather them out of all countries, into which I have driven them in My anger, and in My fury, and in great wrath; and I will bring them back to this place, and I will cause them to dwell safely: and they shall be My people, and I will be their God; and I will give them one heart, and one way, that they may fear me forever, for their good, and that of their children after them: and I will make an everlasting covenant with them, that I will not turn away from doing good to them; but I will put My fear in their hearts, and they shall not turn aside from Me. And I will rejoice over them to do them good and I will truly plant them in this land with My whole heart and with My whole soul" (Jeremiah 32:37–41). So long as they are upon it, it is as if they are planted before Me *in truth with all My heart and all My soul*, but when they are not upon it, it is as if they are not planted before Me in truth, not with all My heart, not with all My soul.

Rabbi Shimeon ben Elazar says: Jews in foreign lands are idolaters.[2] How so? There was a non-Jew who gave a party for his son and went and invited all the Jews living in his city, even though they ate and drank of their own provisions and their own attendants waited on them, they were idolaters, as it is said: "Lest thou make a covenant with the inhabitants of the land, and they go astray after their gods and do sacrifice to their gods and call thee, and thou eat of their sacrifice; and thou take

---

[2]In the text of the Talmud, *Avodah Zarah* 8a: Rabbi Ishmael . . . idolaters *in purity*.

of their daughters to thy sons, and their daughters play the har-
lot after their gods" (Exodus 34:15–16).

Excerpts of these *beraitot* from the *Tosefta* in *Avodah Zarah* are
quoted in many places in the Talmud and the decisors[3] and would
appear to be common knowledge. Nonetheless, they call for serious
study, with special regard to their source and the true extent of their
relevance, particularly for the modern age.

Many questions arise when we delve into these words of our
rabbis. For example:

First, their unparalleled sharpness. What was it that could have in-
duced them, based their understanding of the verses (of which there are
yet more) to equate dwelling in other countries with a kind of idolatry?

Second. What difference is there between Abraham, who went
down to Egypt because of famine (Genesis 12:10); Isaac, to whom it
is said: "Go not down into Egypt . . ." (Genesis 26:2) when the famine
was of like severity; and Jacob, who went down with permission to
Horon in his flight from Esau and then to Egypt on account of famine
(Genesis 46:1–7) in fulfillment of the earlier decree (Genesis 15:13)?
And what is the difference between them and Elimelekh and his sons
in the days of the Judges that caused Rabbi Shimeon to speak so
pointedly against him in particular (as quoted by Rambam)?

Third. Where do we find that David actually went out of the
Land? Is it not a fact that *he went to Moab for a brief while only*, to rescue
his family who were being pursued (1 Samuel 22:1–5) *and returned at
once* when commanded by the prophet Gad (ibid.). All this, in fact,
preceded his complaint concerning those who drove him from the "inheritance of the Lord" to "idolatry." By contrast, *after* this complaint,
Scripture records his flight with his men to *Akhish, king of Gath* (1 Samuel
27), it being *that flight alone* that brings him *to dwell in foreign parts* for a
period of one year and four months (ibid., 7, and according to Rashi
there, only four months altogether). Further, *Gad and Ziklag and the*

---

[3]For example: *Avodah Zarah* 8a; *Baba Batra* 91a; *Ketubbot* 110b; Rambam,
Law of Kings 5:9–12, etc.

field of the Philistines are all an integral part of the Land of Canaan ("... which is counted to the Canaanites ..." [Joshua 13:2–3]) *and within the boundary of Israel and the inheritance of Judah* (Joshua 15:31, 45–47). Even Moab is not entirely outside the Land since the promised borders extend even that far, save that God gave it to the children of Lot in their time (Deuteronomy 2:9, as with Ammon and Se'ir). The sages said: Ammon and Moab give the tithe of the poor in the seventh year (*Mishnah*, *Yadayim* 4:3, as *halakhah* handed down by divine decree to Moshe at Sinai. See Rambam, Tithes 1:1, 6, and Radvaz there). Rashi, however, in *Ketubbot* 101b., says concerning David: "... he had to flee from *Eretz Yisrael* to the king of Moab and Akhish the king of Gath." So why, after all, is this considered having left the Land?

Fourth. What is the meaning of the expression "peace-time" as the *Tosefta* uses it: "Anyone who leaves the Land *in peace-time* and goes elsewhere, it is as if he were an idolater," and why should this be the decisive factor? When is it not "peace-time"? Hunger? War? Perhaps *Galut* (Exile)?

And *fifth.* What is the proof that they adduced specifically from the children of Gad and Reuben, and why have the decisors resorted to the prophecy of Jeremiah on the in-gathering of the exiles in connection with these *halakhot*?

All these questions are easily answered and lose their complexity the moment we understand and accept the fundamental principle of Rambam "*that* Eretz Yisrael *means Jewish sovereignty: wherever* Eretz Yisrael *is spoken of* its meaning is those lands conquered by the king of Israel or the prophet *with the consent of the majority of the Jewish people*, and this is what is meant by the expression, *kibbush rabbim* (conquest by the majority). . . ."[4]

---

[4]Tithes 1:2, and compare with Laws of Kings 5:6, and on condition that they first conquered "Eretz Canaan according to its boundaries as specified in the Torah" (ibid., that is, Jewish sovereignty within the borders of the historical *Eretz Yisrael*).

Rambam maintains, of course, that there is in *Eretz Yisrael* a narrow boundary, the land of Canaan (Numbers 34), which is the decreed bound-

Nor can it be argued that Rambam speaks only of a king in the absolute sense—a prophet, a great court, or of the messianic king of the House of David. That is clearly not so, since we see that Rambam speaks of Joshua, who neither founded nor established a royal dynasty in accordance with all the laws pertaining to it and yet whose status, halakhically, was that of a king with regard to all communal functions, especially regarding the conquest of *Eretz Yisrael*. Clearly, Rambam is typologizing the appointment of a king "like Joshua who was appointed by Moses and his court and like Saul and David who were appointed by Samuel Ha-Ramati and his court" (Laws of Kings 10). Such is the view of the sages (*Yoma* 70b and 73b) concerning the question put to the *Urim* and *Tummim*; Rambam (Vessels of the Sanctuary 10:12) rules: "They are not consulted for the ordinary person, but only for the king, or the court, *or one who serves a communal need*, as it is said, [at the appointing of Joshua for the conquest of the Land]: 'And he shall stand before Elazar the Priest [who shall ask counsel for him after the judgment of the *Urim* before the Lord; at his

---

ary, and, in contrast, there are the broad boundaries of the Promise as explained in the Torah (Deuteronomy 18:8–9) in the cities of refuge. This is quite clear in his words (Tithes 1) and is also the opinion of *Kaftor va-Ferah* (chap. 11). For this reason he believes the *mitzvah* of conquest of the Land and its settlement is *dependent and conditioned on* the war with the Seven Nations within the *borders of the Land of Canaan, and that only one mitzvah, not two, can be counted here.* Whereas Ramban, who enumerates two *mitzvot*—to destroy the Seven Nations and their idols, on the one hand, and to conquer and settle the land, on the other—states explicitly his opinion (there in *Sefer ha-Mitzvot*) that *Eretz Yisrael* has only one boundary, which is the Euphrates River (ibid., addenda to the Positive Commandments, 4), that the decreed boundary is that of the verse in Deuteronomy 1:7 and not the boundaries enumerated in Numbers. It cannot, then, be that it should depend on the war with the Seven Nations alone. Rather, it is an independent *mitzvah*. Therefore, according to Rambam, we have two classes of boundary and one *mitzvah*; for Ramban, two separate *mitzvot* and one boundary (cf. Rabbi Joshua mi-Kutna, *Yeshuot Malko, Yoreh De'ah* 66).

word they shall go out, and at his word they shall come in, both he, and all the children of Israel with him, even all the congregation]' (Numbers 27:21); 'he' refers to the king, 'and all the children of Israel' to the priest annointed for battle or '*he through whom the community has to put its question*' (the High Priest) [a combination of the language of the *Mishnah* in *Yoma* with that of the Talmud at the end of chap.7, ibid.], and 'even all the congregation' to the High Court (*bet din ha-gadol*)." Regarding the appointment of judges, Rambam writes (*Sanhedrin* 4:13–14): "The exilarchs in Babylon perform the same role as the king, and they have the right to rule over Israel in every place and to judge them, with their consent or without. . . ." Similarly with every appropriate judge (except that "they do not adjudicate fines"). It is only in connection with the holiness of the Sanctuary, the Temple court, and their annexes that Rambam rule that "only by authority of the king, the prophet, the *Urim* and *Tummim* and the Sanhedrin of seventy-one elders . . ." (The Temple 6:11), and that all of these are prerequisites only for the establishment of the Temple, but not for the conquest of the land. Along these lines, Rabbi Kook has written: "It appears to be the case that when there is no king, since the laws of the kingdom are also relevant to the condition of the people, these rights of implementation of the laws revert to the people in their collectivity. . . .Whoever rules the people is the one who implements the laws of the kingdom, which are the sum of the needs of the people as the world and the times dictate. . . .There's no arguing that even judges, ordained rabbis and the heads of the whole community perform the functions of the king" (*Mishpat Kohen*, Kings 144:15, see esp. p. 337). This view won the approbation of the majority of the luminaries of his generation. Rabbi Herzog and other scholars of his generation also relied on this when they authorized the revival of the State of Israel under the laws of the kingdom, in the Torah-mandated war of 5408 (1948) and those that followed.

That the law of the land comes into force only through the consent of the people is, in fact, spelled out by Rambam (end of Theft 5): ". . . be the king a non-Jew, be he a Jew" (ibid., 11, and we find the same determination in the *Shulhan Arukh, Hoshen Mishpat*, Theft

369:6–7). Rambam stipulates no condition other than the consent of the people of that land alone—not the king's righteousness, fear of God, or spiritual level. This refers neither to an idealistic government nor to that of the Davidic Messiah, but to an actual and legally halakhically prescribed government that can uphold Jewish sovereignty in *Eretz Yisrael*.

This makes very clear the distinction between the patriarchs, whose connection to the land of Canaan was a holy one but not one of sovereignty, who were able to acquire permanent inheritance in it only by dint of extraordinary effort—as with the cave of Makhpelah and the field of Shekhem, who were strangers and settlers upon it. Elimelekh, on the other hand, lived in the days of the Judges, after the conquest by Joshua, when the Jewish people possessed their own land and were secure in their inheritance. The *Tosefta* brings a proof from the children of Gad and Reuben who assisted in the conquest of the land "before God," that is, when the *kedushah rishonah* (first sanctity) took effect, and by virtue of this their inheritance on the other side of the Jordan was also sanctified "before God."[5]

Therefore, David, who fled across the borders of the kingdom while Saul ruled and was obliged to put himself *under protection of foreign kings* of Moab and Gath, *and was dependent on them*, to the degree that he was considered a faithful servant of Akhish the Philistine— all this is implied by *the expulsion from the inheritance of God to serve other gods. For whoever is subjected to the rule of the stranger indeed is like him, a part of him.* If the foreign king is an idolater then indeed all his subjects, all who fall beneath his lordship, are characterized as such, even if their hearts are far removed and they are meticulous in performance of the *mitzvot* and the prayers every day of their lives. All of this is made explicit in the Torah, in Targum Onkelos and the Targum Yonatan ben Uziel, and Rashi. The Torah states at the end of the curses in the Reproof (*Tokhahah*): "And the Lord shall scatter thee

---

[5]Look closely at Numbers 32:20–24, and all places not included in the zone of conquest of those who came up from Egypt were considered as outside the Land at that time for this purpose.

among all peoples, from one end of the earth to the other; and there
thou shalt serve other gods, which neither thou nor thy fathers have
known, wood and stone" (Deuteronomy 28:64). Onkelos translates:
". . . and you will practice idolatry there *to the people*," and Rashi
explains: "as the Targum renders it, not actual idol-worship, but they
pay a poll-tax to the heathen priests." Yonatan ben Uziel elaborates
with the words of David: "they have driven me out this day from
being joined to the inheritance of the Lord," that is, David went
among *a people* who were idol-worshipers (1 Samuel 26:18). It is thus
abundantly clear from where the rabbis derived this statement that
"anyone who dwells outside the Land is as one who worships other
gods."

It is impossible to maintain that all this is only because David,
like Elimelekh, dwelt first among Jews in Bethlehem of Judea, and
from the time that he went to Moab and to Philistia he became assimi-
lated among the heathens. This, in any event, does not agree with the
words of the rabbis, who clearly stated in this regard that "a man
should dwell in *Eretz Yisrael*, even in a city where the majority is non-
Jewish [idolaters], rather than outside the Land and in a city which is
entirely made up of Jews." From this it is clear that what the rabbis so
strongly opposed was that those living outside the Land received protection and placed their dependence on the government of non-Jews.
It appears that when the rabbis state that Jews in the Diaspora are
absolute idolaters, because of "the gentile who made a feast for his
son and invited all of the Jews in his city," they were alluding to the
feast of Ahasuerus, in which the Jews played their part, eating at the
king's expense of prohibited food, from the Temple vessels. Great anger
befell them; yet none of this furthered their cause with Ahasuerus
one inch, according to the commentary of the sages (*Megillah* 11b,
12a, and also ibid. Rashbi!). The *Tosefta* adds that the circumstance
so strongly condemned refers not to the feast of Ahasuerus but to a
regular wedding feast with ritually persmissable food and drink
served by Jews in conformity with the highest and most scrupulous
standards. Nonetheless, the banquet is in essence an opening to inter-
marriage, which, ultimately, leads to idolatry. One cannot say any-

thing to one's children when they see the honor and affection exchanged between Jew and Gentile at such a banquet! And if you argue that surely all this could happen also in *Eretz Yisrael* in a city where there are only Gentiles, then that brings us directly back to the question of sovereignty. In *Eretz Yisrael*, with Jewish sovereignty, *an Israeli is not dependent on the Gentiles*, even in Hebron, which to this day is mostly Gentile, whereas, outside the Land, you are dependent and conequently not free to absent yourself from any city or state event. Even in New York, where so many Jews are to be found, the dependency and proximity have tremendous influence, and thus was dependency on the Gentiles the very life-breath of Jews even in cities in Poland and Russia where they formed the majority until the Oppressor, may his name be blotted out, came and destroyed them. It is a self-evident truth that since the Emancipation, there has been an ever-increasing rate of mixed marriage and assimilation taking place in the Diaspora.

This being so, the obligation of *aliyah* and the prohibition on leaving *Eretz Yisrael* finds its truest and most rigorous application in the words of the rabbis bearing on the sovereignty of Jews in *Eretz Yisrael*, as against their dependency while under the hegemony of a foreign power. This is also the explanation of "peace-time," that is, the sovereignty of Jews in *Eretz Yisrael*. So Rashi explains the statement of Rabbi Papa in the section of the Talmud dealing with fasts (*Rosh ha-Shanah* 18b): "In time of peace—when Israel is not under foreign domination." On this basis we do not rend our garments in mourning for Jerusalem and the cities of Judea since the time that they were restored to the sovereignty of Israel. "'If a man sees the cities of Israel *in its devastation'*; even though Jews live there, *since foreign peoples rule there, it is called devastation.*"[6]

---

[6]Magen Avraham, *Shulhan Arukh, Orah Hayyim* 561:1. Indeed, peace as meaning Jewish sovereignty already appears in the prophecy of Haggai, referring to salvation and redemption when God will break the chariots of the nations: "... and on this place I will establish peace, saith the Lord of Hosts" (Haggai 4:9). Rashi says that this refers to the days of the Has-

It should, therefore, be clear that the essential stringency pertaining to settlement outside the Land and to leaving it applies at a time when there is Jewish rule over *Eretz Yisrael* and when there is an in-gathering of exiles, since then the inheritance of God is actualized ("in the time that they are upon it," in the language of the *Tosefta*). Indeed, the obligation of *aliyah* to *Eretz Yisrael* and the settlement of *Eretz Yisrael* certainly pertains also to the time of Exile, as Ramban has shown in *Sefer ha-Mitzvot* (*Hashmatot* [omissions] to positive *mitzvot*, 4), and as all the decisors have confirmed in their citing of the law embodying the husband's power to coerce his wife, and the wife's to coerce her husband, to make *aliyah* to *Eretz Yisrael* and not to depart therefrom.[7] Even Rambam dealing with the law of the servant stated:

---

moneans (ibid. 4:6). However, in the prophecy of Zekhariah (8), peace is conceived in simple terms, as Ibn Ezra explains the guarantee in the Torah: "'. . . and I will place peace in the Land'—among you" (Leviticus 26:6). Therefore, the abolition of the fasts commemorating the Destruction is dependent on the condition of peace—according to Rashi, external peace, that is, Jewish sovereignty. But if one looks into the response of the prophet Zekhariah (8), it will be seen that the happiness and joy in these days are *conditioned on peace and truthfulness between man and his fellow, that is, in the act of rectification for the sins that caused the Destruction*: ". . . Truth and judgments of peace they adjudged in your cities. And none of you shall meditate evil to your neighbor in your hearts . . . for all these things I have hated, sayeth the Lord" (ibid. 15–17). These failings in the traits of peace and truthfulness among Jews are certainly the most serious causes of the confusions, difficulties, and distress that we endure each and every day in *Eretz Yisrael*, even allowing for all God's mercies and the wonders he has performed for us with the Ingathering of the Exiles taking place before our very eyes.

[7]*Ketubbot* 110; Rambam, Marriage 13; *Shulhan Arukh, Even ha-Ezer* 75. See there, *Pithei Teshuvah*, where he goes to great lengths to refute every responsum obviating the requirement of *aliyah* based on danger, or on the difficulties of *mitzvot* dependent on the Land. He went so far as to rule that one should not heed the court of one's city, and even one's parents, if they oppose his *aliyah*. There does not appear to be anything comparable in any other area of *halakhah*.

"and this law (that the servant can oblige his master to make *aliyah* to *Eretz Yisrael* and oblige him not to depart from there) applies at all times, even now when the Land is in the hand of idol-worshipers."[8]

This obligation in the time of the Exile derives not only from the sanctity established by those who came up from Babylon, which has not ceased, but from the original sanctity of the Land itself, as it was also in the days of the patriarchs. It has for some time now been established by Rabbi Ishtori Haparhi (*Kaftor va-Ferah*, chap. 10, pp. 37–38), that the sanctity of the Land *precedes* the conquest by Joshua, dating from the time of the patriarchs, and in essence from the burial of Jacob in the Cave of Makhpelah, based on his vow and that of Joseph to take up his bones. As Rambam has written: ". . . and that which receives him in life does not resemble that which receives him after his death, and even so the great among the sages would bring their dead there. Go and learn from our forefather Jacob and Joseph the Righteous" (Laws of Kings 5:11). The Hatam Sofer has expounded on this at length (*Yoreh De'ah* 234).

It is also clear that Rambam excluded from the *halakhah* all those opinions that prohibited *aliyah* (*Ketubbot*, ibid. regarding the Three Vows and Rabbi Judah, who said that anyone who goes up from Babylon to *Eretz Yisrael* transgresses a positive commandment, as it is said: ". . . they shall be carried to Babylon and there they shall be *until the day that I take heed of them, says the Lord*" (Jeremiah 27:22; and *Tosafot* there in the name of Rabbi Hayyim Cohen, etc.), for we see that Rambam brings into the *halakhah* half of the words of Rabbi Judah there: "Just as it is forbidden to go from the Land to outside the Land, so it is forbidden to go from Babylon to other lands, as it is said: '. . . they shall be carried to Babylon and there they will remain'" (Laws of Kings 5). Therefore, it is clear that Rambam rejected the first part of his statement and ruled like Rabbi Zera, who escaped from there and went to *Eretz Yisrael*.[9]

---

[8]Servants 8:9. The question remains why he did not cite this as well in Marriage!

[9]Rabbi Haym of Brisk (on Rambam, Kings, ibid.) has already explained that the verse in Jeremiah cannot refer to the second *Galut* for one who rules that "the first sanctity is abolished," as does Rambam.

Even the decisors who have written that in time of Exile there is a *mitzvah* incumbent upon every person to make *aliyah* but not upon the whole of Israel "together and by use of force,"[10] *nevertheless all concede that this condition falls away the moment there exists the right to go up to the Land,* and there is in this no rebellion against the nations. Avnei Nezer explains that if authorization to go up is granted, the obligation for all Israel to do so will return, and, possibly, this corre-sponds to "the day that I take heed of them" (*Yoreh De'ah* 454). He sharply rejects the opinion sent to him that even when authorization exists, *aliyah* is prohibited. And he responds: "Fanciful notions, noth-ing more! And a whole barrage of them will not dislodge the words of Rashi from their place," that only by force is it prohibited. How re-markable is the comment of Avnei Nezer on "the day that I take heed of them," long before it actually came to pass in the generation before this one, in two stages: first, the Balfour Declaration, on November 2, 1917, which authorized the establishment of the national home in *Eretz Yisrael*, followed by the San-Remo Resolution of the League of Nations, in the Spring of 1920 and the UN Resolution and Proclama-tion of the State on 5 Iyyar 5708 (1948). Such Torah scholars as Rabbi Meir Simha, author of *Or Same'ah*, saw in this the annulment of the Vows. The Three Vows were already abolished, as indicated, with the UN resolution on the establishment of a Jewish state in *Eretz Yisrael*, whereas the actual establishment of the state created a new halakhic reality, which allows for *aliyah* and, therefore, the obli-gation of *aliyah*. The essence of the *mitzvah* of *Eretz Yisrael* is fulfilled via Jewish sovereignty even according to those decisors who disagree with Ramban.

On the other hand, even according to the view of Ramban and the majority of decisors siding with him, there is a great difference, as he explicitly indicates in *Sefer ha-Mitzvot* (ibid.), between the fulfill-ment of the *mitzvah* in time of Exile through the *aliyah* of individuals

---

[10]Cf., Rashi, *Ketubbot* 111a. See also the Responsa of Rashbash 2, *Pe'at ha-Shulhan* 1; and Avnei Nezer (*Yoreh De'ah* 154), who has written that every individual who makes *aliyah* fulfills the *mitzvah*, even though there is no obligation to do so because of the Vows.

and their individual settlement of *Eretz Yisrael*, as opposed to the fulfillment of this *mitzvah* in our day, when there exists a Torah obligation on the whole of Israel. In the words of Ramban: "that we have
been commanded to take possession of the Land that God the Most
High gave to our forefathers, and we are not to leave it in the hands
of strangers from among the nations, nor allow it to go waste" (ibid.).
Now this is the fulfillment of the *mitzvah* of sovereignty and of settlement, *hityashvut* in Zionist jargon. Ramban establishes unequivocally
that the non-Jews living there can remain *on condition of nonbel-
ligerence*, and that we will do battle with them only "if they do battle
with us, but *the Land* we will in no wise leave in their hands, nor in
the hands of others of their kind, now or in the future."

As for Rambam, he explicitly defines the sovereignty of Israel
in its land as the essence of the *mitzvah*, as he states: "*Eretz Yisrael*
wherever it is spoken of, is identical with those territories that were
conquered by the king of Israel or the prophet with the consent of the
majority of Israel . . . *and as they are destined to be restored in the third
inheritance*" (Tithes 81:2, 26).

Actually, there is absolutely no argument between Rambam and
Ramban *on this point*, and the whole dispute in the *Sefer ha-Mitzvot* is
only over where to assign the essence of the *mitzvah*. Rambam having
already designated war with the Seven Nations (positive *mitzvot*,
187), and explained at length that *this is a* mitzvah *for all generations*.
According to Rambam, the *mitzvah* of the conquest of the Land and
its settlement *depends* on the *mitzvah* of war with the Seven Nations
(Tithes 1:3). It is, therefore, *all one* mitzvah *of the 613 mitzvot. Ramban,
however, argues with this and maintains that war against the Seven Nations
is distinct from capturing and settling the Land.*

That discussion aside, we return to the crux of our argument,
that in our times the *mitzvah* of upbuilding *Eretz Yisrael* has resumed
its status as a fundamental obligation in the fullest sense of the term.
That which we call "Zionism" is simply the fulfillment of this *mitzvah*
"equal to all the *mitzvot*" through the establishment of a sovereign
state over great portions of *Eretz Yisrael*, her defense, the cultivation
of her barren places and their settlement, wherever this is possible, by

dint of the strength of Jewish sovereignty. The obligation of *aliyah* and the prohibition of leaving also attain their fullest importance and rigor in our time. The great scholar Rabbi Yaakov Emden has written in the introduction to his *siddur* (*Beit Yaakov*—Sulam Beth-El) that prayer *outside the Land directed toward* Eretz Yisrael *is effective only when one cannot go there through force of circumstances.*[11]

Having established that the right and the ability to go to *Eretz Yisrael* in an unimpeded manner—effectively since 5 *Iyar* 5708—creates an absolute obligation to go there according to Avnei Nezer, Rabbi Yaakov Emden, and all of the decisors, *and also according to Ramban and Rambam in consonance with this*, it would surely be strange to find someone turning up in New York, even as a *shaliah* (emissary), and speaking of the obligation of *aliyah* when, in fact, the prohibition of leaving is as serious as the obligation of *aliyah*, as we have seen. On the other hand, how odd are the words heard in the name of some rabbinic scholars, that if they go to *Eretz Yisrael*, they will not be able to leave again and disseminate Torah to their flock scattered throughout the lands, for surely the obligation of settling and the prohibition of leaving are of equivalent force, based on any rigorous reading of Rambam and Ramban. It is true that they consider it a *mitzvah* incumbent only upon one who has the opportunity to perform it, but that applies only in the time of Exile, when there was no unconditional right and clear possibility for every Jew to go to his land.[12] But then, along come other great and prominent sages

---

[11]His words find ample confirmation in the prayer of Solomon: ". . . and pray to Thee towards their land. . . ." (1 Kings 8:48) *only* in relation to their captivity, when they were taken from Israel and set among the nations (ibid., verses 44–45) and all others pray in the Land and in the Temple.

[12]It would be a mistake to think that even today there is no absolute obligation to return, and it is only a *"mitzvah kiyumit"* (to be performed only if and when circumstances allow), since these ideas (from the Rashbash to Avnei Nezer) rely upon the Three Vows for their authority, and these became a dead letter when the Nations agreed to set up a Jewish state in *Eretz Yisrael*, with the support of *the majority of the Jews in Israel and*

who argue: "How can this be so? For if indeed all the competent Jewish educators were to abandon their lives abroad and go up to *Eretz Yisrael*, then in fact all the Jews left behind—and unquestionably many *will* regretably be left behind—will plunge headlong, albeit innocently, into assimilation, and what can we do other than to lament their fate?"

To resolve our dilemma are four wonderful innovations that God enabled man to create in our times: (1) citizenship, passports, and tourist visas; (2) transportation; (3) communications; (4) educational institutions in *Eretz Yisrael*.

Everyone grasps how it is possible to make use of the educational institutions of all types that have arisen in *Eretz Yisrael* for the strengthening of Jews living in other countries, and it is an undeniable fact that wonders are worked in even the short time that a young man or woman spends in Israel, more than by any other kind of educational system with which we are familiar.

It is equally clear that transportation and communications bring the remote near, and that nothing stands in the way of broadcasting from *Eretz Yisrael* to the rest of the world with the same quality and impact that one finds in New York. Somewhat analogously, we learn that we do not proclaim leap years or sanctify new moons abroad unless there is no one to do it in *Eretz Yisrael*: "For *from Zion* goes forth Torah and the word of God *from Jerusalem*" (*Berakhot* 63).

However, the truly unprecedented innovation, within the context of this essay, is that today, as never before save perhaps for certain chosen individuals, such as ambassadors and their entourage, we have citizenship, passports, and tourist visas. Each individual remains

---

the rest of the world, and also the majority of great religious personalities among them. Thank God, the State of Israel came into being. A minority of these great figures and their students do not have the power to uphold the Three Vows against the will of God and the will of the majority of Jews. This also finds expression in the formulation of the Vows: "until you shall desire," and we see that the love for Zion has had the desire to triumph for three generations, with God's help.

a citizen of his country and travels abroad on its passport with a tourist visa. As such, he is not a temporary resident; effectively, he never completely leaves the jurisdiction and authority of his own country. He does not become an immigrant or a temporary resident of the country to which he travels but is registered solely as a visitor. Such a citizen remains bound by all the duties and restrictions of his own country as well as endowed with all its rights and privileges, and can always turn to his country's representatives in the place where he is visiting. Only if he becomes involved in an accident or in criminal activity will the local authorities deal with him. Even then, to be sure, they will notify his country's officials and will act on the basis of reciprocal agreements and, generally speaking, will repatriate him immediately after he is adjudicated or even before. Of course, it is the duty of every tourist and visitor to conform with local custom, for in this we were instructed, as is known: "Why is it that the angels came to Abraham and ate, and why did Mosheh ascend to the heights and not eat?—to teach you, a person should never do otherwise than is the custom of his place" (*Baba Metzia* 86b). The tourist, however, is not a part of the country he visits but remains an inseparable part of the country of which he is a citizen. The rabbis were not dealing with this reality when they established the prohibitions on travel from *Eretz Yisrael* to foreign lands, for we have seen that the severity of the prohibition of leaving was intended in essence to obviate the coming into a state of protection and dependence on a foreign government and society. To do so implies that the visitor may become a part of that country's fabric with effect on him and certainly on his children and grandchildren. In our present case there is no such an act of "leaving." Therefore, an Israeli tourist who travels the world with an Israeli passport has effectively never left *Eretz Yisrael*—as we have seen in Rambam's words that "*Eretz Yisrael*" means the duly representative governmental authority of *Eretz Yisrael*. On the one hand, all Jews are today obligated to go on *aliyah*, and, on the other hand, there is no sin in leaving Israel for someone who holds an Israeli passport and travels with a tourist visa. Only one who *settles*, even temporarily, in a foreign country is considered one who leaves *Eretz Yisrael*.

The prohibitions related to leaving *Eretz Yisrael*, according to Rambam, fall into five degrees of severity:

1. To leave and settle in a foreign land is a major prohibition, and no plea of *force majeure* other than overt and direct life-threatening situations can win exemption. See *Pithei Teshuvah* on *Even ha-Ezer* 76:106, according to the Mabit. This kind of threatening situation exists only when traders are constrained from travel, thus facing imminent poverty. This differs from the situation of the Dispersion or the patriarchs, who came only as outsiders to dwell in *Eretz Yisrael*. Even so, Jacob departed only when explicitly allowed to do so, and Isaac, absent permission, did not do so. Abraham's descent because of famine took place before the land was given to him in particular, since at the terebinth of Moreh (Genesis 12:7) he was told only "*to thy seed* I will give the land." Only when he came up from Egypt, *and after his separation from Lot* east of Beth-El was he told ". . . to thee I will give it, and to thy seed for ever. . . . Arise, walk through the land in the length of it and in the breadth of it; for I will give it to thee" (ibid. 13:14–17). With this, Ramban's criticism of Abraham regarding his descent to Egypt (commentary to Genesis 12:10) falls away, though the hard fact remains that there were consequences, in the sense that "the deeds of the fathers are a sign to the children."[13] Moreover, the patriarchs' going down from *Eretz Yisrael* was to "sojourn" temporarily and not to settle (Genesis 12:10; 26:2–3; 47:4), even though "temporary" has the habit of prolonging itself, and in Jacob's case, translated itself into twenty years. Nonetheless, after the conquest of the Land, Elimelekh, who went to Moab, "forfeited his life to God" (as Rambam has it, Laws of Kings 5:9), and David who was forced to flee for his life, considered himself as one who worshiped idols.[14]

---

[13]See also Maharal, *Gevurot ha-Shem* 87:10.

[14]The most draconian application of the prohibition of leaving *Eretz Yisrael* to live elsewhere concerned going down to Egypt, and I have already proven that in its essence this, too, is prohibited both for the indi-

Therefore, one who goes down from *Eretz Yisrael to settle* abroad, unless he is fleeing for his life or being forced to apostasy, is truly like one who tears himself away from God's mercy and His *Shekhinah,* concerning which the Jerusalem Talmud (*Mo'ed Katan* 6:1) said: "A Kohen came to Rabbi Hanina and said to him: 'What is the law regarding one who goes to Tyre to do a *mitzvah,* to perform *halitzah* or levirate marriage?' . . . He responded: 'That man's brother left the bosom of his motherland *and embraced that of a strange woman, blessed is the Lord who smote him,* and you seek to follow in his footsteps?!'" A similar case we find in our Talmud (*Ketubbot* 111a), upon which Tosafot state, "that case is dealing with one who is not intending to return."[15] Even if they are in mortal pursuit of him or persecuting him religiously, he can only leave for a time "if it is his intention to return," like Jacob. The Talmud further states (*Baba Batra* 91a) that even one who inherits the merits of the patriarchs cannot put his reliance on them once, like Elimelekh, he leaves *Eretz Yisrael* to permanently settle in other lands.[16]

---

vidual *and for the group* who place themselves under the protection of Egypt. Particularly is it a prohibition on the king (*Megadim* 3, "*Derekh Eretz Pelishtim*"). Also from the words of the ruling of Rambam on this, that the conquest of Egypt by a king of Israel acting on the authority of the court is permitted (Laws of Kings 5:5). We therefore have a proof that our approach in this whole area is correct, in principle, for Egypt conquered by a king of Israel is under the rule of Jews and is no longer called "the land of Egypt" delineated in the prohibition.

[15]*Avodah Zarah* 13a, beginning with "*Lilmod Torah velisa isha.*"

[16]I have written at length in another piece ("*Derekh Eretz Pelishtim,*" *Megadim* 3), attempting to prove that even the Torah prohibition of departing and going down to Egypt has its basis in the acceptance of Egyptian protection, which is the opposite of leaving Egypt. Therefore the king specifically has a *mitzvah,* in the words of the prophet Isaiah: "Woe to them that go down to Egypt for help" (31:1). The rabbis unanimously agreed that in the days of Hezekiah they transgressed even though they were still in the Land (*Sukkah* 52).

2. One who leaves *Eretz Yisrael* on a temporary basis, to "sojourn" abroad and not to settle there, that is, he travels on a temporary resident's visa or on condition of acquiring a *temporary* residence or work permit, is subject to all the laws in the Talmud and decisors regarding who is permitted to depart and why. That is to say: He is free to go to learn Torah and to take a wife, these being important *mitzvot* (*Tosafot*), even if there is a place for him to learn in *Eretz Yisrael*, save that he is not happy with his learning there. The same applies to finding a wife (*Avodah Zarah*, ibid., like Rabbi Yosi). The opinion of Rabbi Ahai Gaon, author of the *She'iltot* (Emor, section 103) is that he is free even with respect to any and all *mitzvot*, when there is no practical alternative. This permission extends even to a Kohen, despite the impurity of other lands.[17] In matters left to the discretion of the indi-

---

[17]Rambam has similarly written about the ritual impurity of a Kohen when it affects the performance of other *mitzvot* and there is no practical alternative (Mourning 3:14). However, Netziv (Ha'amek She'ailah, his exposition of the She'iltot, ibid.), restricts the rabbinic sanction to the *mitzvot* involving the study and dissemination of Torah and the honor and dignity of one's fellow-man but excludes the *mitzvot* that are rabbinic in origin, in opposition to the Turei Even (Avnei Miluim to *Hagigah*, beginning "Not for Chaos did he create it; for civilization he created it").

It seems to me, by way of speculation, that the decree of ritual impurity pronounced upon foreign lands was initiated by Yose ben Yo'ezer Ish Tzeredah, and Yose ben Yohanan Ish Yerushalayim (*Shabbat* 15a-b), *who lived during the period of the Hasmonean uprising and were part of the effort against the Gentile government and its influence. When they then threw off the foreign yoke and won independence, they sought to arouse the whole of Jewry in other countries to join them at once in* Eretz Yisrael, *so that the* Shekhinah *should rest upon them* and the influence of the foreign culture on Israel would disappear. This is the understanding of Rashi on the verse in Haggai (2:6): "Yet again, in just a little while—from the time that this Persian yoke sent upon you shall be no more, yet another will arise to rule over you and to oppress you, one of the kingdom of Antiochus, and but a short while will he reign—and I will shake—*with wonders performed for the Hasmoneans*—the heavens, and the earth—*and they will know that my*

vidual, he may go to their fairs, businesses, and legal proceedings, since he is considered a *matzil miyadam*—one who prevents the non-Jew from exploiting some resource (*Avodah Zarah*, ibid.), and not only for the sake of a livelihood but also to increase one's earnings (*Mo'ed Katan* 14a). Only where one goes off "to roam the world and see its sights" have all the sages ruled (*Mo'ed Katan* 14a) *that permission for this is not granted.* All these instances concern one who goes off for a time, brief or extended, with the intention of returning to

---

Shekhinah *dwells in this house*, and they will bring gifts of gold and silver, as it is written in the book of Joseph Ben-Gurion (Josephus)." Now it is clear that, to Rashi, the *Shekhinah* dwelt in the Second Temple *when the Hasmoneans came upon the scene. As independence and self-rule returned to Israel, so the* Shekhinah *returned*, and Rabbi Yaakov Emden in *Mor u-Ketzia* (Part 2) holds that at that time even the *Kedushah Rishonah* (Initial Sanctity) was restored, a conclusion it is possible to draw from the words of Rambam (Tithes, chap. 1, and The Temple, end of chap. 6), that the first sanctification was contingent upon exclusive sovereignty. But here is not the place to elaborate.

It is conceivable that even the rabbis of eighty years before the Destruction, who again passed decrees connected with the impurity of foreign lands and implemented those laws even more strictly were, almost certainly, the Shammai and Hillel who lived in the days of Herod, as is stated clearly in *Shabbat* 17a. They wanted to limit Jewish dispersion and to restrict the foreign cultural influence on Israel, specifically through renewing the building of the Temple, even though eighty years before the Destruction was only a short time *after* Herod had rebuilt the Temple. (He came to the throne in the year 37 of the Common Era. In his eighteenth year he began preparations for the rebuilding of the Temple, gathered all the materials, and prepared everything, and only afterward tore down and built, over a period of one year and five months [Josephus, *The Antiquities of the Jews*, end of Book 15].) This brings us, approximately, to year 15 of the Common Era for the renewal of the Temple, which is about eighty years before the Destruction since, it seems reasonable to assume, we should not include the years of the insurrections themselves in all the calculations of the rabbis. The Zealots' revolt erupted, as is known, in 66 C.E.

Eretz Yisrael (*Tosafot, Avodah Zarah* 14a) and Rambam addresses this most incisively:

> The prohibition of going from *Eretz Yisrael* to other countries is always in place—unless it is to learn Torah, to take a wife, or to stop a non-Jew getting his hands on something *and he will return to the Land*.[18] Likewise, let him go for business, *but to settle there is forbidden*, unless his land was in the grip of famine [or if] he will not make money nor find remunerative work and not have a cent to call his own—let him go where he can make a living. And in spite of the fact that he is permitted to go, it is nevertheless not the act of a righteous man, for we see that Mahlon and Khilyon were two of the greatest of their generation, and only left under duress, *and (yet) their lives became forfeited to the Omnipresent* (Laws of Kings 5:9, emphasis added).

Since, as we have already proven above, in our days when there is a Jewish government in *Eretz Yisrael* and we are free to go there, there is an absolute duty to go.[19] Therefore, one who undertakes a permanent occupation abroad, makes it his home, and has no thoughts of *aliyah*, has the same status as the man who leaves *Eretz Yisrael* with that same motivation. Conversely, one who dwells abroad on a temporary basis, for purposes of business and study, the performance of a

---

[18]In Mourning 83:14, Rambam writes: ". . . for a religious purpose, when no other channel was open to him, for example, that he went in search of a wife or to learn Torah. . . ."

[19]It cannot be argued that living under the protection of a regime that is not idolatrous, as Rambam under the protection of the Muslim Caliph in Egypt, is not transgressing the ban of living abroad; Rambam does not suggest anywhere that it is not prohibited to live under Islamic rule. From this it can be learned that the prohibition is alive and well, because one is considered to be a part of the Gentile regime and its culture, and because of mixed marriages, the threat of which is great, even when they believe in monotheism.

mitzvah, or for any legitimate activity but who intends to go up to *Eretz Yisrael* at the first opportunity, has the same status as one who sets out with such a purpose. The entire distinction between those living abroad who have not gone on *aliyah* and those who go down from the Land rests solely on the notion that the inhabitants of the Land fulfill a *mitzvah* but that there is no absolute duty to go there. This was correct in the time of the Exile, as indicated above, according to Rambam, when *Eretz Yisrael* was not in the hands of the Jews, and at the time of the patriarchs—and even for most of the period of the Second Temple (the period of the Hasmonean Kingdom apart). Yet even then this runs counter to the view of Ramban and the majority of the authorities who support him. Today, however, even this notion is null and void and no longer has any basis in reality.[20]

It might be argued that precisely within the terms that we have demonstrated above, the whole issue is contingent upon the protection of the government, but it is clear that one who resides permanently, or even for an extended period of time, under the aegis of a heathen king, is considered to be like him, like a subject of his kingdom, even if he should weep and wail the livelong day before God. As Avnei Ezer suggests (*Yoreh De'ah*, 457, ibid.), "the ruler of that people," in a manner of speaking, "puts his seal" on all his subjects' prayers, and it is as if an iron curtain separates the expatriate from God.[21] In the modern, enlightened state, however, which believes in God (and not in pagan deities), where there is no religious coercion, and which maintains the separation of religion and state, it is possible to be a citizen without in any way coming under the aegis of "the priests of idolatry," and here there is no transgression whatsoever. Therefore, there are those who say "how fortunate is our lot" that the

---

[20]This is not simply *a mitzvah* to be performed only when circumstances allow, as it was in the times of the Exile—a view held by a number of decisors: Rashbash and Avnei Nezer, and perhaps Rambam, as opposed to Ramban, Rabbi Yehudah Halevi, and all those whose opinions are cited in *Pithei Teshuvah* to the *Shulhan Arukh, Even ha-Ezer*, 75, 6.

[21]See Onkeles and Rashi, Deuteronomy 28.

majority of Jews have found their path, their deliverance, and their redemption in the United States and similar countries, under the aegis of democracy, and they believe that they will always live there—a sentiment shared by many. This can in no way be equated with or deemed proper authorization. First, because even if this kind of residence does not belong in the category of "pure idolatry,"[22] such an individual is nevertheless considered "an inseparable part" of Western and especially American culture, of its religious and cultural atmosphere. Second, the moment one participates as a guest at a non-Jewish function, even in a completely "kosher" one, and is inattentive to what is happening, the upshot may well be mixed marriages, if not in the first generation then in the second or third, as we see almost every day. And third, there is present under all circumstances the positive obligation of *Eretz Yisrael* and its holiness, to go on *aliyah* and settle there; it is only the additional negative commandment against staying outside of *Eretz Yisrael* that is dependent upon alien protection. In any event, every Jew is obligated to be subject to Israeli rule.[23]

---

[22]As Rashi, ibid., explains: "*as if to say without intention and oblivious to the implications.*"

[23]As we have said, it is a great *mitzvah* and even an obligation to take up citizenship in the State of Israel, as provided for by the Right of Return, itself the quintessential expression of our faith in the words of the prophets and in the vision of the Ingathering of the Exiles, and not just to reside in *Eretz Yisrael* as a foreign national. Accordingly, anyone who relies on this approach cannot travel the world with a foreign passport, but only with an Israeli one, except in an emergency situation, such as redeeming Jewish captives and saving Jewish lives. Moreover, the person who becomes a citizen enters into the condition of *a native of* Eretz Yisrael *with all the halakhic ramifications*, whereas the visitor who comes on a tourist visa and a foreign passport remains definitively a foreigner with all of the halakhic ramifications (for example, observance of the second day of a holiday). A resident who is not a citizen and who does not lose the name "alien" is, it seems, of doubtful status. We can decide his case in line with his state of mind: if to make *aliyah* and take up citizenship, once his problems and all that obstructs him have passed, then he is already like a native in all respects and

Finally, like it or not, "the ruler of that people puts his seal on his prayers," and he is far from God. Facing *Eretz Yisrael* in prayer is not worth anything when it is in one's power to go there.[24]

3. One who leaves *Eretz Yisrael* with Israeli passport and tourist visa, of whom it is known and attested to by the authorities of his state, and by those of the state he is visiting, *that he does not transfer allegiance, even on a temporary basis*, has then the status of one lodging overnight, bound by the laws of the place in accord with universal practice, save that he has no rights, no duties, and no status in that place. This person is properly considered *a national of* Eretz Yisrael *who has not left its borders*, and not even a "wayfarer" (*Mo'ed Katan*, ibid.), for clearly in the days of the rabbis there was no such thing as an official tourist. *Such an individual commits no transgression by his travels* and is not considered as "leaving" *Eretz Yisrael*, even though, of course, he does miss out on the holiness of the Land while he is absent from it. This is perhaps the dominant notion, extending even to Torah scholars, who currently do undertake many brief trips, even worldwide travel, and of whom it may be said: if they are not prophets, they are surely the sons of prophets.

It follows then that the moment our tourist begins to make a living and to make his temporary home there, *at that point is he deemed to have left* Eretz Yisrael, as we have explained, and he becomes culpable.[25] Prior to that, though, he is not. Of course, it is true that one

---

observes one day of a holiday. Even if "he intends to return" abroad for a time, this changes nothing, since his root intention—in accord with the obligation established by the law, as we have proven above—is to go up and become a citizen in *Eretz Yisrael*. But, if "he intends to return abroad" and not to go up and become a citizen in the foreseeable future, then *he is in contempt of his obligation* to settle in *Eretz Yisrael* and not to depart, and naturally enough is also considered *an alien* with all its halakhic ramifications. May God bestow upon him a spirit of *teshuvah* (repentence/return), that he should be rescued from this dark notion of agreeing to *voluntary* exile.

[24]See Rabbi Yaakov Emden, Introduction to his *Siddur*.

[25]There is no practical difference between leaving *Eretz Yisrael* in actual fact; entertaining the idea of settling abroad after one leaves, where no

who leaves *Eretz Yisrael*, even for the shortest while, does exist, for
that time, without the holiness of *Eretz Yisrael* and likewise forfeits
the fulfillment of its *mitzvot* and is like one that does not keep a positive *mitzvah* at a time that he could do so. In this respect he is like the
man who takes off his tallith and goes without *tzitzit* and without
kippah who, while certainly not sinning, is bereft of all sanctity. In the
case of our tourist, the impurity of the heathen land works its influence upon him, particularly if he is a Kohen, and even if he is merely
an Israelite from a kingdom of priests. For that there is no remedy,
and whoever indulges his wanderlust armed with an Israeli passport
and tourist visa, although not sinning, does forfeit at that time the
mitzvah and the sanctity of the Land. What he feels upon returning
home, as many have affirmed before him ("How good to be back!")
cannot make up for what he has lost, just as the one who goes a number of weeks without *tzitzit* and *kippah*, and resumes wearing them
with a marvelous feeling of "*teshuvah*." Yet, it is good that he has an
intimation of the joy of the soul resuming its abode in *Eretz Yisrael*.
But, if he sets out on this path for the *good of* Eretz Yisrael, *for its
strengthening and its upbuilding, as most of Israel's emissaries have always
done, or to gather in Jews who are scattered and lost, then the sanctity of*
Eretz Yisrael *broods over him and emanates to him even on his travels*,
even if he is detained abroad for an indefinite time through force of
circumstance, as the Talmud states (*Ketubbot* 75a), on the verse in
Psalms (87:5): "But of Zion it shall be said, 'This man and that was
born in her; and the Most High Himself shall establish her,' whether
it be one born in her or one who aspires to see her." Rabbi Kook excel-

---

physical act is involved; or failing to make *aliyah* with the intention of remaining permanently abroad. In all such cases, the only difference is with
respect to the question of punishment at the hands of men, that is, flogging. *There is no difference in their relation to the heart of the prohibition.*
Rambam has written that one who descends to Egypt violates a negative
commandment but does not incur flogging, as descent alone is not prohibited, whereas a later decision to remain does not involve action, thereby
excluding it from corporal punishment (Laws of Kings 5:8).

lently portrayed this based on his personal experience during World War I.[26]

4. In the case of the individual who dwells abroad for a certain length of time *in the capacity of official representative of the State of Israel, such as in a diplomatic posting,* thus being one who "embodies" Jewish rule in *Eretz Yisrael* and represents it before the world, not only is that person utterly free of transgressions of any kind, but he does a great *mitzvah.* Beyond this *kiddush ha-Shem* (sanctification of God) can come about through him if he succeeds in raising high among the nations, the glory of Israel, God's nation and the land of His inheritance, through his appearance, words, and general conduct.

5. In any case, it is the way of the righteous never to leave *Eretz Yisrael,* regardless of circumstances, and to trust in God always (Ramban on Genesis 12:10, Rambam, Laws of Kings 5:9), as it is written, "And he who trusts in God will be surrounded by righteousness" (Psalms 32:10).

It should be emphasized that all of the above has been according to Rambam, and it is reasonable to assume that Ramban agrees at least in part. However, according to Rabbi Yehudah Halevi, and possibly also according to Ramban and his colleagues, it is forbidden to leave the physical Land, and this is "the way of the righteous."

As for the question of intervention by those who live (temporarily!) outside in the internal political disputes of *Eretz Yisrael,* we find that our sages were explicit in their distinction between the inhabitants of *Eretz Yisrael,* who are known as the "*kahal*" (community), and outsiders, who are designated as "*yehidim*" (private persons): "Said Rabbi Assi: 'In practical *halakhah,* one follows the majority of the residents of *Eretz Yisrael,*' as it is said: 'And at the time Solomon held a feast, *and all Israel with him, a great congregation,* from the entrance of Hamath to the wadi of Egypt, before the Lord our God, seven days and seven days, namely 14 days' (1 Kings 8:65) ... who are called '*kahal*' [the inhabitants of *Eretz Yisrael* from the entrance of Hamath

---

[26]*Orot,* "Eretz Yisrael," *Piska* 4 [6].

to the wadi of Egypt], whereas those who live abroad are not called 'kahal'" (*Horayot* 3a). And such was their view regarding the blessing made on the populace. When one sees six hundred thousand Jews assembled, one says: "Blessed is the Master of all secrets, for no two minds are alike, and no two faces look the same" (*Berakhot* 58a). There it states: "Ulla said: 'We take the view that there is no blessing of the "*okhlusa*" (populace) in Babylon.'" This truly is the amazing secret of our times, that the State of Israel has managed to establish itself, and to develop, and to pass resolutions. As we know, every Israeli has his own opinion and his own physiognomy; every Jew is of royal stock and the descendant of prophets; and each and every one is confident of his righteousness and is not prepared to yield his ground by so much as a hairsbreadth. Nevertheless, through wonders and mysteries, they constitute a populace six times larger than the one that left Egypt, may their number increase! In other countries, every *kehillah* (community), indeed, every individual, is a separate entity, and when they have disputes, they simply assert their perceived autonomy and make their own decisons without even experiencing the necessity of collective decision making. Even when all these Jewish organizations do band together to resolve something or other, on foreign soil, it is almost always the doing of the State of Israel or for her sake. One should remember that only the inhabitants of Israel enjoy the complete benefit and pay the complete price of every decision of the nation in Israel, and therefore only they have the right and the duty to make such decisions.[27]

In conclusion, it is an absolute duty and privilege to go up to *Eretz Yisrael* and to never again depart from there, to form part of the collectivity "*kahal Yisrael*" over which the *Shekhinah* hovers. God triumphs through them and through their works and, all the problems, agonies, controversies notwithstanding, we declare, God be blessed, He from Whom nothing is hidden.

---

[27]This is somewhat analogous to the law that a Jewish king cannot be judged, lest there be a mishap, and since he cannot be judged, he cannot judge others (see Babylonian and Jerusalem Talmud, *Sanhedrin*, chap. 2).

It is permitted to leave Israel temporarily, within the halakhic parameters known to us, as elaborated above, and it is permitted to leave as a traveler, and with an Israeli passport even to roam far afield, even though it is not quite proper to do so, for the holiness of the Land is lost to him when he does so. But if one ventures out for the good of *Eretz Yisrael*, its strengthening, its upbuilding, and to attract its dispersed ones to live there, all the more so, if one functions as a diplomat representing Israel to the sanctification of God's name in the eyes of the nations, this is a great *mitzvah*, and no place is too far for the holy influence of *Eretz Yisrael* to reach him.[28] To some extent the same is true for all who aspire to set eyes upon her and who smart at the estrangement and impurity they sense in heathen lands. And if he goes to settle abroad permanently, or resides there and has no thought of going up at the first opportunity, he is considered part of those nations and their culture, and he forfeits the merit of the patriarchs. Once he eats at the banquets and shares the joys of the Gentile, mixed marriages must ensue, and that very fact is the punishment.

Therefore, someone who dwells in the Diaspora and is involved in education, Torah learning, communal affairs or business, *with the*

---

[28]Nor is there, it seems to me, any difference between a Kohen and an Israelite in all these issues when it comes to acting at the level of the righteous, as above—and not only on account of what the later decisors wrote (*Shulhan Arukh, Yoreh De'ah*, section 372, subsection 1), there being no laws of ritual impurity today, but also in the light of what has been proved in the body of this paper: there is absolute consonance between the words of Rambam on the authorization given the Kohen to become ritually impure when outside the Land, and the law that he records authorizing a Israelite to leave the Land. Quite the contrary, regarding the Kohen, Rambam explains that learning Torah and taking a wife are *examples* of a "religious purpose," in line with the view of the She'iltot, and certainly there are no grounds for saying that a Kohen is treated more lightly than an Israelite. As several discussions in the Talmud (*Avodah Zarah* 13a; *Mo'ed Katan* 14a, in the Jerusalem Talmud there) indicate, they are essentially equivalent (cf. Rambam, end of Mourning 3, with Kings 5:9).

intention of making aliyah *when he can, then let him go at once, rear his family and children in* Eretz Yisrael, *and set out at fixed intervals, on an Israeli passport, to educate, study, or do business abroad, and let him again return home to Israel. It is a great* mitzvah *he is performing and no transgression can be laid at his door.* (And, thank God, modern technology makes this possible.)[29]

As for the domestic disputes in Israel, of course any Jew, wherever he may be, can express his personal opinion, but only the actual inhabitants of *Eretz Yisrael* are called "*kahal*," and only they pay the full price of the decision making. Theirs alone is the privilege and the duty to settle issues qua "*kahal Yisrael,*" according to the majority, in conformity with the laws of the country and *halakhah.*

---

[29]There is room, as I see it, to be stringent in cases that involve leaving the country temporarily to live abroad, whether to execute a mission, to study, or to do business. Entire families with children should not be allowed to leave, except with the specific authorization of the court, given that many cases have already occurred involving children and even entire families who, when they "pitched their tent" there, ended up staying. It would be better by far—and cheaper by far!—that the husband alone (or the wife alone) should go for a few weeks and return home for a week's stay, and repeat the process, so that the children grow up in their natural and proper habitat, *Eretz Yisrael.*

4

A Central
Rabbinic Authority:
Costs and Trade-offs

Arnold Enker

There is a certain measure of ambiguity in the defined topic of this article. In context, and given the word *authority*, I assume that the word *central* is intended to convey also the sense of supreme. That, however, still does not answer the question: central or supreme to what and to whom? Is the proposed rabbinic authority intended to be central to Israel and to Israeli Jewry only or, perhaps, might it be structured so as to be central to world Jewry? And, exactly over what and whom is this body supposed to be supreme? As we shall see, different legislative solutions would be called for, depending upon the choices made in answering these questions.

I have already run somewhat ahead of myself, for these opening remarks assume that we are considering a legislatively established body. That, itself, is a matter that requires further consideration. Modern social systems recognize the existence of voluntarily established bodies that are, nonetheless, central and supreme in the spheres of their competent authority. I have some doubts whether such a voluntary body could function effectively in the case of the orthodox rabbinate, partly because I cannot conceive of any contemporary rabbinic group that would accept a sufficient measure of lay participation in its halakhic functions, such as would be necessary in order to give it broad legitimacy in the public eye. I do want to suggest, however, that there exists a broad range of possibilities that are open for consideration and to suggest the implications of the different choices exercised. In the end, some mix of legal empowerment and voluntarism may turn out to be the best choice, yet even then there is a range of options concerning the proper mix.

Let us consider, then, the question of the rabbinic authority's "centrality." As I have suggested, this is not a self-defining term, and the question necessarily arises: central to whom and to what? One obvious question that comes to mind is whether such a body is to be central to Israeli Jewry only or also central to world Jewry? One might choose to strengthen its universal character by universalizing the procedures by which the authority is elected. Strange as this may sound to us, accustomed as we are to the status quo pursuant to which the Chief Rabbinate is elected by an Israeli constituency alone, I have no difficulty in conceiving a body universally chosen.

Such a choice, it seems to me, has significant implications for the internal structures of the rabbinic authority and for its legal standing in relation to the State of Israel. It would hardly be appropriate, for example, to have American Jews participate in an electoral process that is designed to choose an organ of the government of Israel. The rabbinic authority so chosen would have to have a more universal standing, separate and apart from the State of Israel. The Jewish Agency and the World Zionist Congress come to mind as possible precedents, though it may be that our recent experience with these bodies is not entirely encouraging. In any event, this, in turn, would necessarily mean that the central rabbinic authority so chosen could not have the power that the Israeli Chief Rabbinate has today over matters of marriage and divorce in Israel. Nor could it sit in appellate review of the decisions of the Israeli lower rabbinic courts. These powers would have to be transferred to a distinct and separate rabbinic authority. In other words, one price that must be paid for universal centrality is the relinquishment of some legal supremacy.

One might try to achieve a somewhat different mix of influences and powers. For example, one might establish a central rabbinic authority in Israel, by Israeli legislation, which would have legally enforceable powers in Israel but would have only moral force and influence in the Diaspora. This is the model presented by the current chief rabbinate and may be what the draftsmen of our forum topic had in mind when they defined the issue in terms of a central rabbinic authority "in a modern Jewish state." It would not be unfair to suggest that this is not much more encouraging than the precedents mentioned earlier.

A different issue concerning the meaning of centrality is illustrated by certain decisions of the Israeli Supreme Court concerning the rabbinate's power to grant or deny *kashrut* certification. How narrow or broad is the public that will follow the rabbinic authority's decisions? The particular case that arose before the Supreme Court concerned the eligibility of an establishment for such certification if it dispensed kosher food but also allowed entertainment not deemed religiously suitable, in this case a belly dancer. One fact that emerges clearly from this experience is that the answer to this question concerning the breadth of the audience that will be receptive to the rabbinate's rulings depends in some measure on the way in which the rabbinate chooses to exercise its powers.

The rabbinic authority may choose to take a broad view of its powers and functions and to concern itself with the overall moral climate of the establishment no less than with its kitchen, in which case the public that will guide itself by the authority's rulings will be smaller. Or, it may choose to narrow its concern to the *kashrut* of the establishment's food alone and ignore the propriety of the "entertainment" it offers—in which case its decisions are likely to reach and affect a broader audience. The situation calls for the exercise of some very difficult choices on the part of the rabbinic authority. Denial of certification to such establishments may lead to the long-term result that more people will eat treif.

I am not considering here the legal basis or validity of the court's decisions in these cases. I will come to that later. My point here is that there are certain trade-offs that have to be considered as an internal policy matter to be decided on by the rabbinic authority itself, and that the extent of its centrality is, to a substantial degree, a matter for it to choose, based on a broad view of its functions.

We are all aware of the fact that there are nonobservant Jews who do not accept and follow the rabbinate's rulings unless they have no choice in the matter. The so-called right-wing Orthodox groups, moreover, have their own separate rabbinic authorities whose leadership they follow. We do not, however, so frequently take notice of the fact that there exists a large middle-of-the-road group of people who are not observant in the Orthodox sense but who adhere to the traditions to a larger or lesser degree. This group's obedience to rabbinic rulings may often be up for grabs and may be influenced by the rabbis themselves and the choices they make. A "central rabbinic authority" is not a very significant force if the center is so narrowly drawn that one must squint in order to see it.

The supremacy of our proposed rabbinic authority is an equally loose term that requires some further measure of definition. Supreme in relation to what and to whom? Such a body can be supreme only over those who are by law subordinated to its authority or to others who voluntarily accept its rule. In any event, it certainly cannot be any more supreme than, for example, the supreme court, which is to say that it is not superior to the law of the land that created it. As a creature of the law, our supreme central rabbinic authority is necessarily subordinate to the law. This has come as a rude shock to many, particularly to the rabbis themselves, when they discover that the rabbinate is subject to the secular law just as every other organ of the government.

In practice in modern society, this means judicial review of the rabbinate's activities by the secular law system whose function it is to enforce the centrality and supremacy of the secular law. It also means a very close scrutiny of is activities by the secular courts to assure that they conform to the law and the absence of any great sympathy on the part of the courts to the rabbinate's attempts to apply its authority expansively.

A few brief quotations from the Israel High Court of Justice decision in the Raskin case will illustrate the point. This is the case in which the court ruled that the rabbinate, whose legal function it is to supervise and certify the *kashrut* of restaurants and other establishments that dispense food, is not empowered to deny a *kashrut* certificate to a catering hall that serves kosher food, in complete compliance with the halakhic requirements concerning the preparation and the cooking and serving of the food, but that permitted entertainment at catered functions that included performances by a belly dancer.[1] The court said:

> The granting of a certificate of kashrut is established in a secular law from which the [rabbis] derive their authority to issue certificates of kashrut. In the matter of the issuing of kashrut certificates, the [rabbis'] standing is the same as the standing of any other administrative authority. . . . [T]he fact that, in matters of kashrut, the rabbis to whom the power to issue kashrut certificates was given base their decision on the halakha does not detract from the power of this court to intervene when it is called upon to rule whether the rabbis have exceeded the authority given to them by the law.

Furthermore,

> The law [authorizing the rabbis to certify kashrut] was not enacted in order to enforce kashrut or the duty to observe kashrut. Its purpose is merely to prevent deceiving and injuring those who desire to observe kashrut.

Indeed, the court pointed out that the legal empowerment of the rabbis actually decreased their powers in the sense that we are concerned with here.

---

[1]High Court of Justice case 465/89, Raskin v. The Religious Council of Jerusalem et al., 44 (2) Piskei Din 673.

Prior to the enactment of the law, the granting of a hechsher to food products or to establishments serving kosher food was in the hands of the rabbis, and each rabbi could issue or deny a hechsher according to his best understanding and conscience. Anyone who wanted kosher food could choose whatever kosher food he desired, in accordance with his confidence in the hechsher given to the food by this rabbi or another, while each rabbi issued his hechsher based on his own considerations, without having to justify his considerations. With the enactment of the law, the authority to issue kashrut certificates was restricted to those who are designated in the law. But the law also narrowed the range of considerations that are relevant to the giving of a certificate of kashrut, as explained above, since its goal and its purpose are the prevention of fraud in the matter of the kashrut of food.

In practical terms, then, the price of legal recognition and empowerment is a narrowing of rabbinic autonomy. Which rabbis are more central and supreme? Those who are empowered by the law and enjoy its backing and authority but are limited in the range of considerations that they may take into account in determining whether to issue a certificate or not? Or those who act without legal empowerment but are also free of legal constraints, capable of exercising independent halakhic judgment as their understanding dictates?

It seems to me that the sharpness of the clash between the two court systems in Israel stems from several sources: rabbinic failure to understand the values of the secular legal system, which is the source of its legal authority, such as freedom of choice and procedural due process; the desire of the rabbinate, as any other bureaucratic body, to be independent and free from review and restraint by any other body; and rabbinic culture shock in the face of the thought that the rabbis might be called to account and be responsible to anyone else, let alone to nonobservant laymen.

The rabbis do not appear to realize it, but the series of decisions in which the supreme court placed restraints on the rabbinate's powers does not reflect in any way or stem from any animus toward the rabbinate, to rabbinic traditions, or to Orthodoxy per se. These decisions really reflect the application to the rabbinate of ordinary principles of administrative law, as they have been developed by the court with respect to administrative bodies in general.

During the past forty years, the supreme court has gradually enlarged the scope of judicial review over governmental agencies in a body of law known to the profession as administrative law. This phenomenon has expressed itself in many fields of activity. Very noticeable in recent years has been the court's growing pace of intervention in matters concerning activities in the occupied areas of the Gaza Strip and the West Bank. Whereas, years ago, in the earlier period of the occupation, the court ordinarily retreated in the face of arguments that were advanced in the name of security, today the court is much more likely to intervene and to examine the legality of the activity, to exercise its own judgment whether the claims of security are valid and require the particular action taken. This is only an extreme example, chosen here because of the wide publicity that has resulted from such judicial intervention. But the phenomenon of increased judicial review and intervention encompasses a much broader range of administrative activity. Even the attorney general's decision whether to charge someone with a crime or to decline prosecution, long thought to be as independent a realm of administrative decision making as is possible and free from any judicial scrutiny, has recently been subjected to close judicial review. Indeed, there does not exist any sphere of administrative activity today that is free of such review.

It appears to me that this judicial review of the rabbinate is likely to become more intense as time goes on. One subject that is ripe for examination from the perspective of the secular law is the question of who is competent to exercise the rabbinic functions set forth in the secular law. We are all familiar with the debates over who is a Jew and the judicial decisions concerning this question. I believe that we shall next see a series of cases dealing with the no less difficult question, who is a rabbi? Are rabbinic appointments, with the legal

powers and responsibilities consequent upon such appointment, limited to Orthodox rabbis only? Or, are other rabbis, who have been
ordained by different schools and who adhere to different movements, no less legally qualified to fulfill these posts?

This question concerning the qualifications and legal standing
of non-Orthodox rabbis has been considered by the Supreme Court
in connection with the power to officiate at the marriage ceremony
for Jews. One of the legal functions of the Chief Rabbinate is to grant
recognition to various rabbis to conduct marriage ceremonies. Several Reform rabbis challenged the Chief Rabbinate's refusal to recognize them as so qualified, on the ground that in so acting, the Chief
Rabbinate exceeded its legal authority.

In the particular case at issue, the petitioners' claims were rejected by the Supreme Court.[2] This decision, however, was based in
large measure on quite narrow and specific grounds. The law concerning marriage and divorce declares that the marriage and divorce
of Jews in Israel is to be conducted according to the *halakhah*. Therefore, these Reform rabbis, who petitioned the court to be recognized
and who had expressly declared that they intended to fulfill their
functions—if recognized—in ways that are contrary to the *halakhah*,
had no grounds on which to claim that they were wrongly and ille-
gally disqualified.

As is obvious from the narrow basis of the above decision, another case based on different facts might readily result in a different
decision. There is still room for debate and disagreement concerning
what are the requirements of the *halakhah* in many cases. An obvious
example that readily comes to mind is the marriage of Ethiopian Jews.
At least one Orthodox rabbi in Israel—the Chief Rabbi of a city in
the center of the country—is prepared to marry them. Suppose a Reform rabbi declared his willingness to marry Ethiopians. It is difficult
to see how his candidacy could be rejected on the grounds accepted

---

[2]High Court of Justice case 47/82, The Fund for the Reform Movement
in Israel et al. v. The Minister for Religions, 43 (2) Piskei Din 661.

in the above mentioned decision, namely, that he was prepared to solemnize marriages contrary to the *halakhah*.

Furthermore, this ground for the decision is good with respect to rabbinic qualification to conduct marriages. It cannot be sustained, however, with respect to other rabbinic functions that the secular law declares are not to be governed by the *halakhah*. One should not necessarily assume that the governing substantive rules are those of the *halakhah* merely because the matter at issue is a religious function. Once again, in the eyes of the secular law that has created the chief rabbinate and that defines its powers and functions, the rabbis are civil servants, governmental functionaries who are part of the administrative bureaucracy that was created to provide various services to the public.

The debate over who is a Jew proves the point. Religious conversion is clearly a religious function. Nonetheless, the requirement in the law that one born of a non-Jewish mother and having converted to Judaism in order to be recognized as a Jew has not been given a religious definition, let alone the Orthodox religious understanding. Even in the context of marriage, there is room for debate—on the secular legal level—whether the requirement that marriages be governed by the *halakhah* concerns the halakhic permissibility of the marriage or its halakhic validity. The distinction has significance, for example, with respect to the marriage of a kohen to a divorcee or to a convert. A reading of the Supreme Court decision concerning the Reform rabbis makes it clear that some judges are prepared to interpret the term "*halakhah*" quite broadly.

A similar problem is likely to arise at some point in the future with respect to the question of who is qualified to participate in the selection of the Chief Rabbis. The law provides that a certain number of electors are to be chosen from among the local rabbis throughout the country—the chief rabbis of the principal cities and of various other cities and local neighborhood rabbis with an equal number of electors chosen from various other sources that do not necessarily encompass only observant Jews. A smaller number of electors is appointed by the minister for religions. While this last group of electors is small in number, it is clearly a significant group that could hold the balance of power in close cases.

Most of the time, the position of minister for religions has been filled by a representative of the National Religious Party. This party, however, may be weakened in the future for various reasons, including the possible influence of the large immigration from the former Soviet Union. Political interests that have as one plank of their platform the development of greater religious pluralism have already expressed their interest in this post, even before the recent large immigration from these areas. If these groups win this ministry, the minister's power to appoint these electors can change the face of the Chief Rabbinate.

Apart from such political considerations and possibilities, we find in recent years still further legal developments that might bear on the issue of defining qualified electors. The first of these developments concerns the question of whether a woman may serve in this capacity. Again, to the great displeasure of the official rabbinate, the Supreme Court ruled recently that women should serve as electors of the Chief Rabbi for Tel Aviv–Jaffa, and the same clearly holds for the Chief Rabbinate.[3] One could hardly expect any different decision from a civil court that is guided by general legal criteria that prevail in the society at large. The rabbinate may be free to determine such qualifications by itself, without outside interference, so long as it is an independent body whose authority is based on voluntary acceptance by the public that is loyal to it. It cannot expect, however, to be free of such generally accepted restraints so long as it derives its authority, not to speak of its budget and enforcement powers, from the secular law.

Even more significant is the line of precedents concerning the makeup of the various religious councils throughout the country. Here, too, the courts have intervened to open up membership on such councils to women.[4] More significantly for our immediate pur-

---

[3]High Court of Justice case 953/87, Poraz v. Shlomo Lahat, Mayor of Tel Aviv–Jaffa, et al., 42 (2) Piskei Din 309.

[4]High Court of Justice case 153/87, Shakdiel v. The Minister for Religious Affairs, 42 (2) Piskei Din 221.

pose are the court decisions that brought into these councils persons who are other than strictly Orthodox in practice and identification, all in the name of ensuring a fairer and more equal distribution of membership so as to be more representative of the general public at large and of those who make use of the services provided by the religious councils.[5]

It is possible to distinguish between the religious councils and the electors of the Chief Rabbis. The religious councils are not in themselves religious bodies and lack the authority to perform religiously signifcant acts or to pass on questions of religious law. Their function is to allocate budgeted funds to various communal bodies in order to provide as broad a range of religious services as is possible to all those in the general community who wish to benefit from such services. Therefore, it is argued, their composition should include representatives of all persons who are interested in obtaining such services, and they should not be comprised of Orthodox people exclusively. The Chief Rabbis, on the other hand, rule on religious questions according to the *halakhah*, so the body that selects the rabbis should be constituted of persons who accept the *halakhah*'s mandates and live by the *halakhah* in their personal lives.

This argument, however, is not entirely convincing. At stake here is the composition of the body of electors that choose the Chief Rabbis, not the qualifications of the rabbis themselves. There is no provision in the law requiring that such electors be observant Jews. Indeed, as we have seen, the law provides that almost half of the electors are chosen from sources that are such as to render it likely that many of them will not be observant. Historically, too, many of these electors have, in fact, not been observant. So there is no reason to assume that the appointees of the minister for religions, who hold the balance of power, must by law be observant or will necessarily be so. The very opposite is the case.

---

[5]For example, High Court of Justice case 65/76, The Likud Party in the Petach Tikva Municipality v. The Minister for Religions, 30 (2) Piskei Din 836.

It is not for me to resolve here the issues relating to rabbinic responsibility in contemporary society. This is obviously, in large measure, a matter of personal outlook and preference. What is important here is to note the issues and to understand the choices. The multifaceted nature of the concept of supremacy and centrality suggests that accountability does not necessarily result in the diminution of influence. Less accountability may result in greater power, but that is likely to be exercised over a narrower segment of the community.

We have all witnessed, to our deep chagrin, the consequences of the mixing of the chief rabbinate, personal ambition, and partisan politics. All of the sides involved have undoubtedly suffered therefrom, though it seems to me rather obvious that the rabbinate has suffered the most and has been the bigger loser. This is only natural since the public's expectations from the rabbinate differ from the standards by which it judges political leaders.

The criticism leveled by the Orthodox community itself, that the Chief Rabbinate has lost its autonomy vis-à-vis the state, seems to me to be harsher and more far reaching in its consequences. I have no doubt that the halakhic validity of certain very controversial rabbinic decisions can be defended with ample citation of chapter and verse. The public perception, however—whether accurate or not—that the independent exercise of halakhic judgment and discretion in these matters may have been compromised, as part of an election deal, has undoubtedly weakened the chief rabbinate's standing in some circles.

The political element in the selection of the Chief Rabbis in our generation did not spring out of nowhere. Earlier elections were not entirely divorced from politics. Political involvement is not entirely bad. It broadens the rabbinate's constituency and contributes to the selection of candidates who command wide appeal. It also imposes obligations on those who participate in the selection process, who might not otherwise feel themselves bound by the rabbinate's pronouncements.

Still, one has the sense that the proper balance has not been so evenly maintained in more recent times. The difference may be due, in part, to increased competition between the different Orthodox groups and their respective political parties. In other words, the successful establishment of a central and supreme rabbinic authority by means of the law may depend upon our ability to create structures that will make the rabbinic authority answerable to the public but, at the same time, insulate it from partisan politics.

5

The Israeli Chief Rabbinate: A Current Halakhic Perspective

Aharon Lichtenstein

Whoever formulated the topic to which I have been asked to address myself—"The value and place of a central rabbinic authority in a modern Jewish state. Is there halakhic significance to a central rabbinic authority in a democratic state?"—manifestly saw the issue of the status of the *rabbanut ha-rashit*, Chief Rabbinate, as related to its existence within a sovereign modern and democratic context. I readily concede that this factor is, quite conceivably, of genuine importance. However, it can only be considered after one has dealt with the prior (both logically and historically) question of the role of a central rabbinic authority per se. What, we ask ourselves, is the halakhic significance, if any, of a *rabbanut rashit* in any context?

That issue is itself to be analyzed with respect to two levels: the requisite and the optimal. We must first ask ourselves whether the establishment of a central rabbinic body and subsequent acknowledgment of its authority is normatively mandated. Even if we should determine, however, that it is not, it may still be contended that the existence of such an institution is desirable as an instrument toward the realization of clearly perceived halakhic—and not merely social or even moral—desiderata.

As regards the first level, we must obviously differentiate between a possible obligation to found a *rabbanut rashit* in the first place and the duty to abide by its dicta once, by whatever means and for whatever reasons, it has been firmly established. The case for the former presumably rests upon the precedent of the Sanhedrin—whose institution the Rambam posited as the initial phase of the *mitzvah* of setting up a judicial system rather than as its culmination: "How many regular tribunals are to be set up in Israel? How many members is each to comprise? First there is a supreme court holding sessions in the sanctuary."[1]

Not surprisingly, Rabbi Kook implicitly drew upon the comparison. In a brief essay written just prior to the founding convention of the *rabbanut ha-rashit*, he expounds his conception of its prospective role and character; and, citing the verse that the Rambam[2] had adduced as proof that the classical *semikhah* could be reinstated, he issues a clarion call: "The revival of the rabbinate means the return of the glory of the rabbinate. Is this not an echo of the prophetic voice that assured us: 'And I will reinstate your judges as at first and your advisors as in the beginning.'?"[3]

From a rigorous halakhic perspective, however, the analogy is just that: a suggestive model that may be regarded as embodying certain elements and, hence, as positing certain values but as having no direct normative relevance. The Sanhedrin[4] was a formally constituted body that, ideally, both provided general spiritual leadership

---

[1]*Mishneh Torah* (MT), *Sanhedrin* 1:3.

[2]*Perush ha-Mishnayot* (P.H.), *Sanhedrin* 1:3.

[3]"Hator," 14 *Adar* I, 5681; reprinted in *Ha-Rabbanut ha-Rashit le-Yisrael be-Avar u-va-Hoveh* (Jerusalem: Shorashim, 1973), p. 7.

[4]Generically, the term includes both the central body of seventy-one and smaller council/courts of twenty-three. Within this essay, it is ordinarily used only with reference to the former.

and was invested with wide-ranging legislative and judicial authority—and this, with respect to the Diaspora as well as to *Eretz Yisrael*.
In the Rambam's succinct formulation:

> The Supreme Court in Jerusalem represents the essence of
> the Oral Torah. Its members are the pillars of direction; law and
> order emanate from them to all of Israel. Concerning them the
> Torah assures us, as it is written: "You shall act in accordance
> with the directions they give you" (Devarim 17:11). This
> is a positive command. Anyone who believes in Moses, our
> teacher, and in his Torah, must relate religious practices to them
> and lean upon them.[5]

Clearly, no modern counterpart exists—or, under present conditions, can exist. Membership in Sanhedrin was confined to those
who had been ordained as a link in an unbroken chain of *semikhah*
going back to Mosheh Rabbenu's investiture of Yehoshua. The Rambam[6] held that the institution could be restored, even in pre-Messi-
anic times, but only under conditions, such as the overwhelming
consensus of the foremost *talmidei hakhamim* of *Eretz Yisrael*—which
neither currently obtain nor are anticipated on the horizon. Contemporary halakhic sanction for a national rabbinic authority must be
sought, then, without regard to the classical Sanhedrin.

That precedent aside, no solid base for the mandatory establishment of such a body exists. Not only does the *halakhah* fail to pre-
scribe such a course at the national level, but, to the best of my
knowledge, it does not even require it at the local level. We are very
much attuned to the concept of *mora d'atra*, a single rabbinic figure or
group endowed by a specific community with spiritual hegemony;
and indeed this model was prevalent in much of the Diaspora and,
historically, served *knesset Israel* well. However, the halakhic status of
the *mora d'atra* related to his position in the wake of his selection.

---

[5]*Mamrim* 1:1.
[6]*P.H., Sanhedrin* 1:3; MT, 4:11.

Nothing militated the creation of the post *ab initio*. It is true that the Ramban maintained, in light of the wording of the verse, "You shall appoint for yourselves judges and officers, tribe by tribe, in every settle-ment God has given you," that each tribe is to appoint its own central *bet din* (court). However, as he clearly indicates, this is, in effect, a miniature Sanhedrin—"Just as the Great Sanhedrin is appointed over all the courts of Israel so one court is appointed over each tribe "[7]—and, hence, of no direct normative relevance to our discus-sion. The earlier part of the *pasuk* does, of course, mandate the ap-pointment of a *bet din* in every locale, but it makes no reference to the need for a single overarching communal authority, either existing solely or as the pinnacle of a spiritual or even juridical hierarchy.

On the contrary, from the *Gemara* it would clearly appear that several *batei din* can coexist in the same town. It speaks, for instance, of litigants' rights to choose between "the courthouses of Rabbi Huna and Rabbi Hisda," both of these being, as Rashi explains, "in one place."[8] Or again, in delineating the scope of the prohibition of "You shall not gash yourselves," which, *inter alia*, Hazal interprets to in-clude an injunction against divisiveness, "You shall not make sepa-rate groups," Abbaye and Rava treat its parameters with respect to contradictory *pesakim* issued by different local *batei din*—taking it for granted that several may exist in the same community, with none designated supreme.[9] A *fortiori*, then, there need be no single super-

---

[7]*Devarim* 16:18.

[8]*Sanhedrin* 23a. I have here assumed the view of Rashi that both *batei din* were in the same town. *Tosafot*, s.v. "*kegon*," held that they were in the same general vicinity but at a distance of at least three *parsa'ot* (approxi-mately seven miles)—but this not because *Tosafot* insisted upon unitary jurisdiction but due to consideration of *kevod harav*, as Rabbi Huna had been Rabbi Hisda's *rebbi*.

[9]*Yevamot* 14a. See also *Siftei Kohen*, *Yoreh De'ah* 242, subs. 10 of the concluding summary. The *Arukh ha-Shulhan*, *Yoreh De'ah* 242:57, states that since it is now common universal practice to elect a local *rav*, others may not engage in *pesak* in his town. But he does not state that such an election is mandatory.

nal national rabbinic authority. Again, it is entirely conceivable that the decisions of such a body, once chosen, may be normatively bind-ing; but its initial designation is, ordinarily, purely optional.

This by no means suggests, however, that the matter is religiously neutral. No spiritually sensitive person, much less a *ben Torah*, can countenance the proposition that, beyond the mandatory, nothing matters. Surely, a halakhic chasm divides a *devar mitzvah* from a *devar ha-reshut*; but the latter, too, can be of considerable spiritual moment. It may be judged more contextually than normatively—but judgment, in the light of halakhic categories, is nonetheless significant. At this level, then, we may weigh the impact of a central rabbinic authority upon halakhic interests—often related to the pragmatic but hardly identical with them—with respect to the various functions of the rabbinate; and this, with an eye to both the constant aspects of the problem and its manifestation within the contemporary Israeli context.

Rabbinic functions are many and can be variously classified. For our purposes, they can best be divided into two broad categories, as they relate to the communal and personal sectors, respectively. Main-tenance and supervision of halakhically related services; develop-ment of religious institutions; public Torah instruction; representa-tion of the religious sector in relation to others, or, of the general Jewish community vis-à-vis its Gentile counterpart; concern for the Jewish character of the Jewish street—all form one cluster of roles. Others clearly address themselves to the individual: participation in rites central to the life cycle; harnessing him or her to halakhic obser-vance; provision of pastoral guidance or support. Still others straddle both realms. *Pesak* may be either public or private, depending upon the substance of the question, the channel of query, and the mode of response. General spiritual influence and inspiration clearly has a dual impact, sensitizing *yahid* and *rabbim* alike. Finally, moral initia-tive clearly relates to both realms. At one level, the enactment of the prophetic mandate, "Execute the judgment of truth and peace in your gates"[10]—understood in both its broad general sense and, in

---

[10]*Zekhariah* 8:9.

Hazal's[11] vein, as a specific call for settling litigation via amicable compromise—provides a measure of personal relief even as it, concur-
rently, promotes communal harmony. At another, commitment to
hesed—regarded by Rabbi Hayyim of Brisk[12] as *the* cardinal rabbinic
obligation—both sharpens social conscience and enhances the quality of individual lives.

Surveying this spectrum with reference to our problem, we in-
stinctively sense a functional relation between the public component
and the advisability of centralization. On the whole, the instinct is
sound, although not uniformly so; it clearly applies to the supervision
of *kashrut*, for example, more than to the instruction of Torah. While,
to many, the issue is debatable even with regard to largely administrative sectors (the equivalent of the familiar arguments for community
control as opposed to distant and faceless big government can be
readily harnessed), in this area, the case for a central authority, with
the scope and weight attendant upon it, is palpably strong—all the
more so, as, within a modern socioeconomic context, the problems
transcend narrow geographic bounds and are not readily amenable to
local jurisdiction. Admittedly, this does not necessarily militate for
regarding centralization as the sole option. A measure of cooperation
between various rabbis or rabbinic groups or some loose confedera-

---

[11]See *Sanhedrin* 6b.

[12]When his eldest son, Rabbi Mosheh Soloveitchik, assumed his first
post as a *rav*, Rabbi Hayyim told him that the primary rabbinic task was
zu tohn hesed. For all the remark's interest and significance, I trust it is self-
evident that it needs to be viewed in context and hardly to be confused
with presumably identical positions expressed by contemporary liberal religious thinkers. While the emphasis upon social justice is common, the total perspective is not. Rabbi Hayyim, of course, took rigorous halakhic
commitment, as well as its role as the basis of social ethics, for granted, and
certainly had no doubts about the significance of a rabbi's duty to sustain
it. His comment was unquestionably impelled by a sense that an increasingly defensive pre–World War I Lithuanian rabbinate had lost its balance
in one direction. He would have been no less critical of reverse imbalance.

tion might constitute viable alternatives. Nevertheless, with respect to the public sphere, the merits of centralized authority are manifest.

Ishut provides a clear example. Hazal demanded that, "whoever does not know the nature of divorce and marriage should not have any dealings with them,"[13] and they set a rather high standard for what constitutes sufficient knowledge. Although they addressed themselves to the individual, obviously there is a public need for safeguards to ensure that those who lack the expertise do not, out of irresponsible indifference or ignorance of their own limitations, involve themselves in this sensitive area. To this end, a central authority can be enormously helpful. Conceivably, the safeguards could be alternatively provided, as in the medical and legal fields, by voluntary professional organizations; and a community can admittedly sustain itself, as in most of the Diaspora today, in their absence. The potential contribution of a central authority is nonetheless self-evident—not to mention its invaluable assistance in coping with the sheer administrative difficulties, such as the maintenance of adequate and reliable records in an age of great mobility.

With respect to other sectors, however, the balance of pros and cons shifts perceptibly. It is not for naught that the Torah postulated that judges are to be posted *bi-she'arekha*—in *Eretz Yisrael*, in virtually every hamlet.[14] Presumably, this insistence was not intended solely to

---

[13]*Kiddushin* 6a, according to Rashi's interpretation.

[14]The *Mishnah, Sanhedrin* 1:6, states that a community must have a minimal population of 120 in order to qualify for a small sanhedrin, but it does not state that the establishment of such a sanhedrin is mandatory. Moreover, the explanation cited in the *Gemara, Sanhedrin* 17b, for the number seems to suggest that it must include almost one hundred who can serve as *dayanim*. However, the Rambam, *Sanhedrin* 1:2, states that the establishment is indeed obligatory and, moreover, omits the explanation (which, in light of the term *keneged* he evidently regarded as symbolic)— conveying the impression that any 120 would suffice. In any event, this requirement does not apply to a simple *bet din* of three, which, in *Eretz Yisrael*, must be set up even in smaller settlements. In the Diaspora, however, *batei din* need only be established in each province; see *Makkot* 7a.

afford easy access to judicial redress. It likewise ensures spiritual leadership that is organically related to its ambient society, aware of its
problems, and sensitive to its needs; that can communicate effectively
with its constituency in light of direct knowledge of its existential
milieu; that can, intelligently, assign priorities and impose demands
while yet aware of limitations; that can serve as a transcending spiritual mentor even as, like The Shunamite Woman, "amongst my people I
dwell."

Bi-she'arekha relates to both the appointment and the exercise
of spiritual leadership. The benefits of rabbinic independence in attain-
ing and maintaining a position are obvious. In many cases, however,
whoever is not responsible to a community is also not responsive to
it. At times, a stance of defiance (although not of insouciance) is
of course desirable. Over the long run, however, the patient wisdom
needed by a spiritual leader to stimulate the spiritual growth of a
community, his ability to speak, and its readiness to listen are enhanced by knowledge that he has been its choice—without external
pressures and *sans* remote-control politicization.

Yet, this is not to suggest, of course, that selection of a *mora d'atra*
can be regarded as a purely sociopolitical matter, wholly independent
of definitive standards. According to the prevalent view, the *halakhah*
has, classically, posited *semikhah*, defined by the Rambam as "the
appointment of the elders to judgeship,"[15] as a prerequisite to serving
on a *bet din*—to membership, that is, in a body that, in *Hazal*'s time and
beyond, constituted the primary seat of local rabbinic authority and
the matrix of communal spiritual leadership. That has, however, only
served to qualify a person to occupy such a post, enabling him to sit on
an ad hoc constellation or to be a candidate for a more permanent
position that the *semikhah* per se had not conferred upon him. Who,
then, determines which *samukh* assumes a specific position is, to the
best of my knowledge, nowhere spelled out in the *Gemara*. If, however,
intuitive judgment and prevalent historical practice are any guide, the
community within which he is to serve seems the most likely choice.

---

[15]*Sanhedrin* 4:3.

Yet, appreciation of the significance of the communal factor in no way obviates the possible role of a central authority in rabbinic appointment. The process can be both general and local—licensing, in accordance with proper objective standards, being assigned to one level, and selection to another. Halakhically, to be sure, *semikhah* need not be central at all. Any group of three *semukhim*—on the Rambam's view, even a single *samukh* joined by two non-*semukhim*[16]—can confer the title. Moreover, according to the Rivash,[17] licensing was only necessary with respect to classical *semikhah*. That tradition having been terminated, every qualified and knowledgeable person can now serve as a *moreh horaah*. Nevertheless, a median course of essentially dual appointment *can* be adopted; and, under present circumstances, may be deemed as highly warranted. The need for maintaining standards and assuring reasonable qualification in all major respects is palpably greater today than in medieval Spain or in the sixteenth-century setting of the Rama who cited the Rivash with apparent approval. That function can perhaps best be consigned to a hopefully disinterested central authority. "Shall a priestess not be the equal of a hostess?" The concern for standards so properly endemic to secular professions can hardly be ignored in the Torah world; and to this end, a central body can be most effective.

Given a measure of goodwill and readiness to prefer the general interest—admittedly rare qualities when both ideology and power are at stake—analogous cooperative accommodations should probably be attainable, *mutatis mutandis*, in other areas as well. However,

---

[16]*Loc. cit.* Generally, the performance of functions requiring *semikhah* is limited to a *bet din* comprised wholly of *semukhim*. Evidently, in this case, the function per se does not require *semukhim*, and the need for even a single *samukh* derives from the specific content of the act of investiture as the transmission of authority. See *Hiddushei Maran Riz Halevi, ad locum.*

[17]See *She'elot u-Teshuvot ha-Rivash*, resp. 271; see also the Rama in *Yoreh De'ah* 242:14. The Rivash agrees that some authorization may be generally required but for incidental reasons—out of deference to a master or to confirm that one can express himself clearly.

one sector is presumably not so amenable and needs to be singled out for special discussion. At a primary level, *halakhah* is avowedly plural-istic. Within certain limits, it not only entertains but also encourages diverse views, and the world of halakhic discourse is animated by the sense that "these and these are the words of the Living God." At a sec-ondary level, however, discourse is to issue in decision, presumably authoritative and definitive; and the diversity that, in the *bet ha-midrash* is regarded with admiration, becomes, in *bet din*, the object of aver-sion. *Mahloket*, the very stuff of which so much Torah study is made, translates, in the context of *pesak*, into divisive dissent. In its stead, univocal summary decision, optimally typified by the Sanhedrin, is posited as ideal.

The implications for centralization are clear. Technically, this discussion may be deemed as irrelevant to our present situation in-asmuch as the formal Sanhedrin is long defunct. Nevertheless, the axiological aversion to divisiveness may very well be in order. At one level, we might take note of the status of the *zaken mamre*, of whom the *Gemara* says that, even if the Sanhedrin whose decision he had countermanded wishes to remit him, it is unauthorized to do so, "that contention might not increase in Israel."[18] Admittedly, one might contend that, given the existence of a central authority, its defiance is indeed punishable as subversion, but that the existence of compet-ing decisions or even contradictory codices is not deplorable per se. However, this contention, probably questionable in any event, is clearly undercut by the *Gemara*'s lament over the fact that, "When the students of Shamai and Hillel whose studies were not complete became many, dissension multiplied in Israel, causing the Torah to become like two Torahs."[19] Clearly, the concern here is not with *lese majeste* but with fissure in the halakhic universe.

---

[18]*Sanhedrin* 88b.

[19]*Loc. cit.*, quoted from the *Tosefta Hagigah* 2:4 and *Sanhedrin* 7:1. The whole question of fundamental attitudes toward diversity and controversy has, of course, deeper roots and broader implications than can here be treated adequately.

Pushed to its logical conclusion, this position militates for a single universal rabbinic authority—for the establishment, that is, of a Sanhedrin or its equivalent. Some have indeed regarded this vision, animating the essay previously cited, as Rabbi Kook's ultimate semi-mystical aspiration upon the founding of the Chief Rabbinate in Jerusalem.[20] Failing that, however, one could still yearn for maximal uniformity within a broad geographic area—at least for adherents of the same ethnic tradition.

Individualists of course bridle at this prospect. Bristling over both possible personal constraint and public atrophy, they regard the concentration of authority as a potential threat—all the more so if they have cause to be circumspect or even suspect with regard to those in whose hands it might be concentrated. Sanhedrin they often regard as a unique institution, effectively relegated to a remote ideal past or envisioned as part of a utopian future but of little relevance, even as a model, to the present. Rabbi Hayyim's refusal, early in this century, to join—and implicitly be subordinated to—a nascent *Mo'ezet Gedolei ha-Torah* is typical. Electricity having then been recently introduced to Brisk, he observed that it presumably represented real progress. Yet, he noted, one could not ignore a disturbing factor. Previously, if a kerosene lamp was extinguished in one location, no other was adversely affected. Henceforth, however, if a failure were to occur at the power station, the whole of Brisk would be plunged into darkness.

Nevertheless, the merits of uniform *pesak* are varied and weighty; and recurrent historical attempts to attain it, whether through discourse and decision, or, as in the case of the *Shulhan Arukh*, by dint of personally molded consensus, illustrate this amply. Moreover, one might particularly press this cause with respect to *Eretz Yisrael*—and this, not in the light of Zionist ideology, but for sound halakhic reasons. With reference to *pesak*, the concept of place is assigned considerable weight. Thus, with reference to the *issur* of "Do not cause fac-

---

[20]See Menaham Friedman, *Hevrah Vedat* (Jerusalem: Yad Izhak Ben-Zvi, 1978), 110–11.

tionalism," Abbaye holds that it only applies to factionalism in a single town but not to conflicting norms propounded or practiced in different towns.[21] Or again, the *Gemara* states that if a *posek* adheres to a minority view, even if he permits what, according to the prevalent position, is prohibited *mi-d'oraita*, his license may be relied upon by members of his community.[22] By extension, the use of the phrase "in his place" notwithstanding, it is entirely conceivable that the relevant concept is as much sociological as geographic. Could not a lone *Habad hasid* in Melbourne rely upon a lenient decision of the Lubavitcher *rebbe* even though he is poles removed from Eastern Parkway?

If this be the case, one may contend that, for our purposes, the whole of *Eretz Yisrael* constitutes a single locale. And this, on the basis of the famous *Gemara* in *Horayot*, which postulates—with reference to defining the community whose collective transgression by a majority of its constituents will obligate offering "a bull sin-offering for an inadvertent communal sin"—that only residents of *Eretz Yisrael* are included in the category of *kahal* (congregation): "Rabbi Assi said: In [the case of an erroneous] ruling [of a court] the majority of the inhabitants of the Land of Israel are to be taken into account. . . . From this it may be inferred that only these are included in the 'congregation' but those are not."[23] The formulation is primarily negative and is intended to exclude Diaspora Jewry. It also, however, bears a positive aspect and expresses the conviction, of both halakhic and philosophic moment, that residents of *Eretz Yisrael* are uniquely bound by a dimension of community absent elsewhere. Hence, the

---

[21]See *Yevamot* 14a.

[22]See *loc. cit.* Of course, this option only exists so long as the point at issue has not been debated and definitively decided by a vote of the Sanhedrin.

[23]*Horayot* 3a. While the *Gemara*'s statement relates to a single *halakhah*, it obviously has major haskafic implications, and it has also been applied to other halakhic areas as well. See, for example, Rambam, *P.H., Bekhorot* 4:3, and *Avnei Nezer, Orah Hayyim* 314.

admonition against *mahloket* and the quest for univocal central authority are doubly meaningful with respect to *eretz ha-kodesh*.[24]

In theory, quite possibly. In fact, however, as we turn to examine
the current state of the Chief Rabbinate in Israel, one wonders how
much of the foregoing is truly relevant. The contribution of the *rabbanut ha-rashit* to the administration and supervision of areas crucial
to halakhic existence is obvious. Equally self-evident, however, is the
fact that, as a quintessentially *rabbinic* authority—whether as spiritual leadership in the broader sense or with regard to the specific area
of *pesak*—it now carries relatively limited weight. Secularists and
haredim largely ignore it, while the non-Orthodox actively fight it.
Its status in the *dati-leumi* community is more secure, but, even there,
many offer it little more than honorific lip service, having recourse to
it only at their convenience. Moreover, as it has become increasingly
regarded as the virtual patrimony of a dominant faction, its base of
support has narrowed, and the number of those who truly look to it
for guidance has dwindled. Even within the world of *yeshivot hesder*,
there are not many who, confronted with conflicting *pesakim* of the
rabbanut ha-rashit and, say, Rabbi Shlomo Zalman Auerbach, would
routinely prefer the former.[25]

---

[24]The emphasis upon the more thoroughly organic nature of Jewish
existence in *Eretz Yisrael* as a factor to be reflected in the structuring of
spiritual life runs as a prevalent strain through Rabbi Kook's address before
the founding convention of *rabbanut ha-rashit*, a contemporary newspaper
account of which (most of it, a literal rendering) is reprinted in Aryeh
Morgenstern, *Ha-Rabbanut ha-rashit le-Eretz Yisrael: Yissudah ve-Irgunah*
(Jerusalem: Shorashim, 1973), 179–80.

[25]Within the religious (*dati*) or traditional (*mesorati*) Sephardic community, the standing of the Chief Rabbinate is relatively higher—but this is
largely, I believe, because of a perceived link between the *rabbanut ha-rashit*
and the centuries-old office of *rishon le-tzion*. This is evidenced by the fact
that the overall stature of Rabbi Ovadia Yosef, who continues to lay claim to
the latter title long after leaving Hechal Shlomo, is manifestly higher than
that of his successor.

I trust I have not overstated the case. Within religious Zionist circles,

Nor, halakhically, is there any reason why they must. In an address delivered before the Mizrahi in the mid-fifties, the Rav, z"l, vigorously upheld the authority of the Chief Rabbinate, as he cited several instances to prove that, historically, even when greater *talmidei hakhamim* resided in his community, a *mora d'atra* had been its final halakhic arbiter. Whatever may have been the case then, it is surely difficult to apply this principle today, for the status of a *rav rashi* as *mora d'ar'a d'Yisrael* is precisely what is in question. Champions of a central rabbinic authority must still wrestle with the crucial question of *mi be-rosh*—who is defined as such, by whom, and how. When there is reasonable consensus about the appointive procedure, the status can be readily conferred and assume halakhic force. In its absence, however, the title rings hollow.

As previously noted, it is entirely possible that even if the choice of a central authority be optional, if a community has decided to create the post, decisions of its occupant may become binding. That only obtains, however, so long as the institution, and whoever is invested with its power, is truly recognized. Royal authority, *de jure*, rests on a social base, *de facto*, so that the *Yerushalmi*[26] states that during the six months that David spent in flight in Hebron, he did not enjoy full regal status. One may question the extent, if any, to which the principle would apply to the spiritual hegemony of a properly constituted Sanhedrin. It is reasonable to assume, however, that it

---

the *rabbanut ha-rashit* certainly does enjoy a significant measure of prestige and a *rav rashi* carries a perceptible aura. His appearance at any *dati-leumi* Torah institution would be regarded as an event by its students and staff, myself included. Yet the sense of genuine general authority or sustained acknowledged leadership is still lacking. The point is readily exemplified by the failure to establish either Yom Yerushalayim as a truly national day of rejoicing or the Tenth of Teveth as a memorial day for the Holocaust. (The account herewith presented was originally written during the tenure of the previous Chief Rabbis and is not fully applicable to the incumbent *rabbanim*. Nevertheless, the basic situation is quite similar.)

[26]*Horayot* 3:2.

does apply to a spiritual mentor lacking this formal designation—certainly so, if the loss of effective control had preceded his investiture.

There is little doubt that the Chief Rabbinate is not presently master of what it regards as its own domain. To its proponents, it is a proto-messianic precursor. To many, however, it is either anachronistic or premature. One may celebrate this fact or lament it; but I do not see how it can be questioned.

Ought we, then, conclude that a moribund *rabbanut rashit* should be dismembered with dispatch? Categorically not. Quite the contrary; if the institution did not exist, it—albeit in possibly different form—would have to be invented. Within a complex modern Jewish society and state, an apparatus to administer and supervise the halakhic aspects of the public sector and to license those who operate within it is clearly invaluable; and it must be staffed and headed by competent and committed persons whose authority transcends narrow bounds. Moreover, on certain public issues, the state, qua collective agent, needs recourse to a definitive *posek*. The princely—some might say, the quasi-papal—aspect is less crucial. It is even arguable that there can be a *rabbanut rashit* without Chief Rabbis. In this vein, some have suggested that the network of *batei din* as a rabbinical court system should be maintained but that the central rabbinate, as an overarching spiritual authority, should be dismantled. Nevertheless, this element, too, surely serves constructive purposes—either by positing a visible human symbol of the state's link to traditional Judaism or, beyond pomp and circumstance, by providing a ready spokesman and forum for it.

What certainly needs to be reduced, however, is politics, bureaucracy, and, above all, illusion. These are, of course, by no means peculiar to the Israeli rabbinic establishment, but they are particularly perturbing when encountered in the Torah world. The political connection is dual. There are internal—at times, internecine—struggles between various groups over power and influence, extending to involvement in appointive processes at the local level. These are generally deplorable but understandable—partly inevitable, and, at times, genuinely *le-shem shamayim*. In addition, however, there is excessive engagement in the broader political process. To be sure, the current official ban—often ignored in practice—against any *dayan's* speaking out on sociopolitical issues, even when these have clear moral import, on the grounds of judicial impartiality, is totally at variance with Jewish tradition and its conception of communal leadership. When, however, a Chief Rabbi becomes embroiled in negotiations over the composition of the Mafdal's electoral list, he tarnishes both the party and his post.[27] Can anyone imagine the Archbishop of Canterbury publicly determining who should be the Conservative candidate in Sheffield?

Moreover, even when matters of clear conscience are at stake, one often wishes for a greater measure of discrimination than, at times, currently obtains. Certainly no one would suggest that the *rabbanut ha-rashit* should wholly avoid advocating controversial positions out of concern for cultivating its self-image as a truly national institution. Yet, in the choice of issues to be addressed and emphasized, a modicum of prudence and a sense of priority is surely in order. Whatever one's own views, one can understand and respect the impetus to align the Chief Rabbinate with radical opposition to territorial compromise. To say the least, advocacy of *af shaal* engenders a factional image—but all recognize that the issue is major, and its confrontation arguably well worth the damage. The Nakash affair—in which the *rabbanut* served as a prime vehicle of opposition to the extradition of a convicted Jewish killer of a French Arab, on several highly dubious grounds—is quite another matter. I trust that even those who enlisted in the crusade at the time, recognize, in retrospect, that the passion for righteousness that impelled it should have been tempered by a greater degree of prudence and sensitivity. In their absence, the *rabbanut's* stature suffered significantly.

Of bureaucracy, presumably little needs to be said, as it is the Achilles' heel of centralization. It should be noted, however, that, in

---

[27]Of course, in some parties such matters are routinely determined by *gedolim*. They act, however, as masters of an avowedly partisan bailiwick who have not been formally invested with a presumably national mantle.

our case, two complicating factors exist. First, many who work within the *rabbanut*'s system lack, by dint of their education, the training and the inclination to promote efficiency. Second, much of the population that perforce encounters the system does not acknowledge its basic tenets, so that the spiritual price collectively paid for its failings is magnified.

As to illusion, I have not the slightest intention of impugning the integrity of those associated with the current Chief Rabbinate. I do not believe they, or their predecessors, have, in any way, sought to mislead the public. There is, however, a measure of self-delusion— fed, in part, by quasi-messianic fervor. The wish being grandfather to the thought, the *rabbanut ha-rashit* revels in seeing itself as that which perhaps ideally it should be but, at present, palpably is not, and, in the foreseeable future, is unlikely to become—a central vehicle for the realization of the prophetic promise: "For Torah issues from Zion and out of Jerusalem comes the word of God." Of this, the *rabbanut ha-rashit* is, at most, an earnest; and it is best that this fact be acknowledged. A *rabbanut* with a leaner self-image and less grandiloquent tone would also be healthier.

As this article draws to its conclusion, the reader will have noted that relatively little has been said of "a democratic state" or even of "a modern Jewish state." Not by accident. To my mind, the link between centralization and democracy, while real, is, within our context, limited. On the one hand, the basic issues related to the inherent conceptual tension between a focal center and *bishe'arekha* obtain even within a theocracy. How authority is divided, whether jurisdiction is hierarchical, who makes appointments, which *pesakim* are binding—these, and similar questions, exist independently of the overall governmental system. Having opted for a given political structure, a religious community may still choose between Presbyterian and Congregationalist models—or something intermediate.

On the other hand, abolition of the Chief Rabbinate would still leave us confronting problems arising out of the conjuncture of halakhic tradition with a pluralistic society and state. In some way, *gittin* and *gerut* would still have to be afforded or denied recognition,

locally if not centrally, albeit perhaps less definitively; and the problem of the non-Orthodox would still be with us. Poor rapport between
the rabbinic fraternity and much of the population would continue
to bedevil us—at least, for some time. Tensions arising out of the
meshing of religion and state would not disappear, nor would coer-
cive legislation be more sympathetically received. If these problems
are to be confronted, far more radical measures must be considered—
with their concomitant, and possibly exorbitant, costs. The thesis that,
in a pluralistic society, there is a trade-off between power and influence, at least at the spiritual plane, and the concurrent contention
that, in contemporary Israel, too much of the latter is being sacrificed
for the former, bears directly upon the established *rabbanut ha-rashit*.
It is advanced, however, by its advocates, with regard to the religious
community as a whole.

Of course, I readily acknowledge that relating the problem of
centralization to its specific contemporary context does bear upon its
analysis. The impact cuts both ways. On the one hand, the friction
attendant upon contact with what is perceived as the heavy and distant hand of central ecclesiastical authority is exacerbated by a liberal and largely secular context; and the exclusiveness more likely to
be accorded a central rabbinate may seem less justifiable within an
avowedly pluralistic order. Within such a context, the difficulty of
building and sustaining a broad base of support for the *rabbanut
ha-rashit* is virtually intrinsic—particularly as Israeli society becomes
increasingly polarized. Rabbi Kook's dream related to the specifically
national aspect of the Chief Rabbinate—to the dimension of *mamla-
khtiyut* so prized by religious Zionism. That dimension entails, however, a presumed relation to a broad social spectrum and the ability to
speak for and to divergent cultural and ideological sectors. Within
the highly charged atmosphere of Israeli religious life, that ability has
proved very elusive—and for obvious reasons. Sociopolitically, very
few can presently remain firmly anchored within the Torah and *yeshivah* world—to whom, to some extent, the *rabbanut* looks for creden-
tials and legitimization—on the one hand, while developing genuine
rapport with the general secular community, on the other. The ma-

jestic stature of Rabbi Kook, combined with his very special background, enabled him to come close, but, of his successors, no one else has done so consistently.

The problem is, at the practical level, graphically illustrated by the elective process. The Chief Rabbis are, in effect, elected by (and must presumably appeal to) an assemblage that includes many anxious to see them steer a vigorous course and others—ranging from *dayanim* who barely recognize the existence of the state to thoroughgoing secularists—who would be happy to see them neutralized. Currently, moreover, the difficulty is further aggravated by both growing polarization and the alienation of many younger Israelis who find Torah Judaism simply irrelevant.

On the other hand, from a halakhic perspective, it is arguable that a strong *rabbanut rashit* is needed all the more in a democratic state precisely because of its weight as a countervailing force to help sustain the state's Jewish character. Moreover, in at least one respect, the modern mindset is more attuned to a central halakhic hierarchy than its predecessors. During the gestation of the Chief Rabbinate in *Eretz Yisrael*, it was the secularists who insisted upon the establishment of an appeals court—an institution some traditionalists regarded as halakhically shaky but which was *de rigueur* to a Western sensibility.

The modern component is surely relevant, then, to a proper consideration of rabbinic centralization—as the ambience of contemporary Israeli society inhibits its development in one respect and yet stimulates it in another. All I am suggesting is that we refrain from exaggerating its significance. If I am thus also correspondingly constricting the significance of this paper, that is a small sacrifice to bring for truth.

Contributors

Rabbi Yoel Bin-Nun, a founding settler of Alon Shvut and Ofra, directs the Ulpana Girls' High School in Ofra and leads the National Guidance Center for Tanakh at the Yaakov Herzog Teachers Institute of Yeshivat Har Etzion in Alon Shvut.

Rabbi Shalom Carmy teaches Jewish Studies and philosophy at Yeshiva University and is the Consulting Editor of *Tradition*. Among his works is the forthcoming fourth volume in the Orthodox Forum series, *Modern Scholarship in Talmud Torah: Contributions and Limitations*, to be published by Jason Aronson Inc.

Rabbi Aharon Lichtenstein is *Rosh Yeshivah* of Yeshivat Har Etzion and the Gruss Institute, RIETS. He is a frequent contributor to books and journals of contemporary Jewish thought.

Dr. Arnold Enker is Professor and former Dean of the Faculty of Law at Bar-Ilan University. He specializes in criminal law, with particular emphases on Jewish criminal law and comparative criminal law, and on professional ethics.

Dr. Eliezer Don-Yehiya is Professor of Political Science at Bar-Ilan University. He has written many books and articles on religion and politics in Israel. Most recently, he edited *Israel and Diaspora Jewry: Ideological and Political Perspectives* (Bar-Ilan University Press, 1991).

Dr. Chaim I. Waxman is Professor of Sociology at Rutgers University and Visiting Professor at the Azrieli Graduate Institute for Jewish Education and Administration of Yeshiva University. Among his books are *America's Jews in Transition* (Temple University Press, 1983) and *American Aliya: Portrait of an Innovative Migration Movement* (Wayne State University Press, 1989). His most recent book, *Jewish Baby Boomers*, is being published by State University of New York Press.

Index

About the Editor

Dr. Chaim I. Waxman is professor of sociology at Rutgers University and visiting professor at the Azrieli Graduate Institute for Jewish Education and Administration of Yeshiva University. Among his books are *America's Jews in Transition, American Aliya: Portrait of an Innovative Migration Movement,* and *Jewish Baby Boomers.*